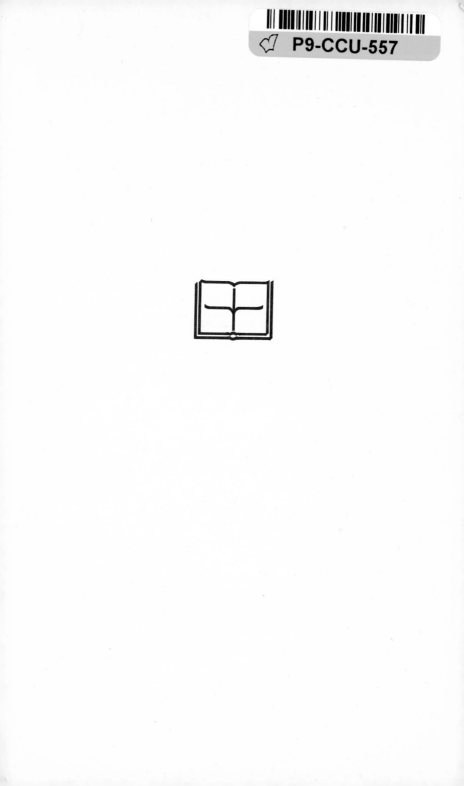

NEW TESTAMENT MESSAGE

A Biblical-Theological Commentary

Wilfrid Harrington, O.P. and Donald Senior, C.P.

EDITORS

New Testament Message, Volume 19

JAMES & JUDE

Richard Kugelman, C.P.

Michael Glazier, Inc.
Wilmington, Delaware

MICHAEL GLAZIER, INC.
1210   King Street
Wilmington, Delaware 19801

Library of Congress Catalog Card Number: 80-68084
International Standard Book Number
    New Testament Message series: 0-89453-123-9
    JAMES & JUDE: 0-89453-142-5

Typography by Robert Zerbe Graphics

Printed in the United States of America by Abbey Press

CONTENTS

EDITORS' PREFACE

New Testament Message is a commentary series designed
to bring the best of biblical scholarship to a wide audience.
Anyone who is sensitive to the mood of the church today is
aware of a deep craving for the Word of God. This interest
in reading and praying the scriptures is not confined to a
religious elite. The desire to strengthen one's faith and to
mature in prayer has brought Christians of all types and all
ages to discover the beauty of the biblical message. Our age
has also been heir to an avalanche of biblical scholarship.
Recent archaeological finds, new manuscript evidence, and
the increasing volume of specialized studies on the Bible
have made possible a much more profound penetration of
the biblical message. But the flood of information and its
technical nature keeps much of this scholarship out of the
hands of the Christian who is eager to learn but is not a
specialist. *New Testament Message* is a response to this
need.

The subtitle of the series is significant: "A Biblical-
Theological Commentary." Each volume in the series, while
drawing on up-to-date scholarship, concentrates on bringing to the fore in understandable terms the specific message of each biblical author. The essay-format (rather than
a word-by-word commentary) helps the reader savor the
beauty and power of the biblical message and, at the same
time, understand the sensitive task of responsible biblical
interpretation.

A distinctive feature of the series is the amount of space
given to the "neglected" New Testament writings, such as
Colossians, James, Jude, the Pastoral Letters, the Letters

of Peter and John. These briefer biblical books make a significant but often overlooked contribution to the richness of the New Testament. By assigning larger than normal coverage to these books, the series hopes to give these parts of Scripture the attention they deserve.

Because *New Testament Message* is aimed at the entire English speaking world, it is a collaborative effort of international proportions. The twenty-two contributors represent biblical scholarship in North America, Britain, Ireland and Australia. Each of the contributors is a recognized expert in his or her field, has published widely, and has been chosen because of a proven ability to communicate at a popular level. And, while all of the contributors are Roman Catholic, their work is addressed to the Christian community as a whole. The New Testament is the patrimony of all Christians.It is the hope of all concerned with this series that it will bring a fuller appreciation of God's saving Word to his people.

Wilfrid Harrington, O.P.
Donald Senior, C.P.

The Letter of James

AN INTRODUCTION
TO JAMES

THE EPISTLE of James had a very difficult time winning acceptance into the New Testament Canon of Sacred Scripture. Even today its presence among the sacred books is an embarrassment to some Christians.

The First, and authentic, Letter of Clement of Rome written to the Church of Corinth about 96 A.D. contains fourteen passages so similar in thought and language to passages of the Epistle of James that some New Testament scholars have concluded that Clement probably knew and used James' letter. If that conclusion were true, then we would have evidence for the existence of James' Epistle before the end of the first century A.D., but this would not warrant the conclusion that Clement regarded James' Epistle as Sacred Scripture. Moreover, the similarities between James and Clement may be due more probably to the dependance of both on the same sources, the hortatory literature of Judaism (the Wisdom literature) and the ethical teaching of early Christianity. The few similarities between James and First Peter, and also between James and First John, are due quite certainly not to any interdependance but to their dependance on the same tradition. The Shepherd of Hermas, a Christian writing composed between 130-150 A.D., also contains a dozen passages, reminiscent in vocabulary and concepts of James' letter. But none of these parallels is conclusive for postulating a literary relationship between the two writings.

The earliest evidence which we have for the existence of James' Epistle is found in the writings of Origen, the third century Christian scholar of Alexandria in Egypt. He cites Jas 2:26 as Scripture and twice he introduces his references to the Epistle with the phrases: "As James the Apostle says" and "the Apostle says." But Origen hints that not all the churches of Alexandria recognized and read James' Epistle as Sacred Scripture. The great doctor of the church, Athanasius, Bishop of Alexandria, lists the Epistle of James in the Canon of Sacred Scripture which he promulgated in 367 A.D.

Eusebius of Caesarea in Palestine, the fourth century church historian, places the Epistle of James among "the disputed books" because not many of the ancients mentioned it and some churches still refused to accept it as Sacred Scripture. Eusebius himself held the Epistle to be canonical because it was being read publicly, i.e. in the liturgy, in many churches. St. Cyril, Bishop of Jerusalem (+386 A.D.) also accepted James as a biblical writing, and St. John Chrysostom, the great doctor of the church and Patriarch of Constantinople (+407 A.D.), wrote a commentary on James.

The East Syrian Church was the last hold-out against the admission of James into the New Testament Canon. The Syrian version of the Bible called the Peschitta, i.e. the commonly accepted Syriac translation of the Scriptures, which dates from the early fifth century A.D., contains the Epistle of James.

The Epistle of James is absent from the oldest extant canon of the Roman church, the famous Muratorian fragment, which must be dated shortly after 155 A.D. None of the early Christian Latin writers of North Africa seem to have known the Epistle. It is never mentioned nor used in the writings of Tertullian, Lactantius or St. Cyprian of Carthage.

St. Hilary of Poitiers (+367 A.D.) regarded the Epistle as an inspired biblical writing and attributed it to the Apostle James. Ambrosiaster (i.e. pseudo – Ambrose) about 350 A.D. cites Jas 5:20 with the remark "as the Apostle James says in his epistle." But it was above all the influence and authority of St. Jerome and of St. Augustine which finally dispelled the doubts of Western Christendom concerning the apostolic authority and biblical status of Jas. Jerome's identification of James, the Lord's brother, who was the reputed author of the epistle, with the apostle James of Alphaeus (a very questionable identification) seems to have been very influential for the admission of the Epistle into the New Testament Canon of Western Christendom. The authority of Augustine also influenced this decision. Augustine wrote a commentary on Jas, which unfortunately has been lost, and in the second of his four books on Christian Teaching (*De Doctrina Christiana*) he uses Jas as a New Testament writing and takes for granted its apostolic authority.

The authoritative influence of Saints Athanasius, Chrysostom, Jerome and Augustine and also the fraternal communication which existed among the churches of the fourth and fifth centuries finally led both Eastern and Western Christendom to accept as Sacred Scripture the twenty-seven writings which comprise the New Testament Canon. The biblical status and apostolic authority of all these writings remained uncontested until the sixteenth century.

Erasmus of Rotterdam, the great Renaissance scholar, while recognizing the canonicity of Jas, questioned its attribution to James, the Lord's brother. The quality of the Greek of Jas is very good – too good it seemed to Erasmus to have been written by the Palestinian from Nazareth, James, the Lord's brother. The author of Jas has an excellent command of the Greek language. He writes

Greek as his mother tongue. He knows and employs Greek rhetorical artistry and his Old Testament was the Greek version used by Greek speaking Jews and Christians of the Hellenistic world. Cardinal Cajetan, the commentator of St. Thomas' *Summa Theologica* and an excellent Greek scholar also rejected the traditional opinion that James the Lord's brother wrote the Epistle.

Martin Luther seized upon the conclusion of Erasmus because he wanted to shake the authority of the Epistle for doctrinal reasons. Luther read Jas as a flagrant contradiction of the Pauline doctrine of utterly gratuitous justification by faith. In 1522 A.D. he wrote in his "Preface to the New Testament" that unlike the Gospel of John, 1 John, Romans, Galatians, Ephesians and 1 Peter, which are books "that show you Christ," "St. James' Epistle is really an epistle of straw . . . for it has nothing of the nature of the gospel about it." (In calling Jas an "Epistle of Straw" Luther had in mind Paul's statement in 1 Cor 3:10-15 concerning the divine judgment on the quality of every teacher's contribution to the building up of the Church, the Temple of God. Jas, according to Luther, would not endure the fire of God's judgment.) Luther lists his objections to the apostolic authority of Jas in his "Preface to the Epistles of St. James and St. Jude." "In the first place, it is flatly against St. Paul and all the rest of Scripture in ascribing justification to works." "In the second place, its purpose is to teach Christians, but in all this long teaching it does not once mention the Passion, the Resurrection, or the Spirit of Christ." For Luther this was a decisive argument against the apostolic authority of Jas because "it is the office of a true apostle to preach the Passion and Resurrection and office of Christ." Luther also criticizes the Epistle's lack of order. James, he says, "throws things together so chaotically that it seems to me he must have been some good, pious man, who took a few sayings from the disciples of the apostle and tossed them off on paper. Or it may have been written by someone on the basis of his preaching."

Luther, however, recognized the ethical value of Jas. In the same "Preface to the Epistles of St. James and St. Jude," from which the preceeding quotes were taken, he writes: "Though this epistle of St. James was rejected by the ancients, I praise it and consider it a good book, because it sets up no doctrines of men but vigorously promulgates the law of God." And at the conclusion of his Preface to James he notes: "for there are otherwise many good sayings in him."

But Luther was never really reconciled to the presence of Jas among the sacred books of the New Testament Canon. Twenty years after he had written his Preface to the Epistle of James he spoke of Jas in an intemperate and exaggerated outburst that has been published in his "Table Talk." "We should throw the Epistle of James out of this school (the University of Wittenberg) for it doesn't amount to much. It contains not a syllable about Christ. Not once does it mention Christ, except at the beginning. I maintain that some Jew wrote it who probably heard about Christ but never met him. Since he heard that Christians place great weight on faith in Christ, he thought: 'wait a moment! I'll oppose them and urge works alone.' This he did. He wrote not a word about the suffering and resurrection of Christ, although this is what all the apostles preached about. Besides there's no order or method in the epistle."

For Lutherans the Formula of Concord, drawn up thirty years after Luther's death, harmonized the apparent contradictions between Jas and Paul's letters in the manner proposed by Melancthon, a harmonization which Luther had refused to accept. So the Epistle of James is still in the New Testament Canon of the Reformation Churches including the Lutheran.

For Catholics any doubt about the biblical status of Jas. was allayed by the Council of Trent which solemnly reaffirmed by name the canonicity of all the writings contained in the Vulgate version of the Bible.

The Epistle of James is a sacred book of the New Testament. It is God's word addressed to believing Christians and they must hear and heed it just as they listen to the four gospels and the epistles of Paul.

The Lutheran New Testament scholar Krister Stendahl, Dean of Harvard University Divinity School, and the late Emile Sander, professor of New Testament at Yale University, concluded their critique of Jas in the article, "Biblical Criticism," *Encyclopedia Brittanica, Macropaedia* Vol 2, p. 969: "The Letter of James, though often criticized as having nothing specifically Christian in its content apart from its use of the phrase 'the Lord Jesus Christ' and its salutation to a general audience depicted as the twelve tribes in the dispersion, is actually a letter most representative of early Christian piety. It depicts the teachings of the early Church not in a missionary vein but to a church living dispersed in the world knowing the essentials of the faith but needing instruction in everyday ethical and communal matters with traditional critiques of wealth and status."

Jas is an excellent example of biblical hortatory literature. It belongs to a literary category called parenesis, i.e. moral exhortation. The author explicitly cites the Old Testament only three times (Jas 2:8, Lev 19:18; Jas 2:23, Gn 15:6; and Jas 4:6, Prv 3:34). But his writing throughout echoes the language of the Psalms, the Prophets (especially their denunciation of social injustices), the books of Proverbs, Wisdom and very frequently what appears to have been his favorite Old Testament writing, the deutero-canonical book Ecclesiasticus, called also the Book of Sirach.

His principal Christian source is the ethical teaching of Jesus such as we find it expressed in the Sermon on the Mount in Mt and in the Sermon on the Plain in Lk. Almost half of James' Epistle, forty-six of one hundred and eight verses, echoes Jesus' teaching as it is recorded in the gospels. Twenty-two of these forty-six verses are very similar in language and concepts to sayings of Jesus recorded in Mt or in Lk (cmp. e.g. Mt 5:11-12 and Jas 1:2,12; Jas 1:5,6 and Mt 7:7; 21:21; Jas 1:22; 4:17 and Mt 7:24,26. Jas 2:5,13 and Lk 6:20; Mt 5:7; Jas 5:12 and Mt 5:33-37). Like the gospels and other New Testament writings James attaches a pejorative meaning to the word *kosmos*, the world. This pejorative use of "world" so frequent in the New Testament is never found in the Old Testament (cf. e.g. Jas 1:27; 4:4; Mt 18:7; 1 Jn 2:15-16). Very probably the author of Jas drew from the same tradition of Jesus' teaching as did the evangelists who compiled the Sermon on the Mount (Mt) and the Sermon on the Plain (Lk). He may have used the collection of Jesus' Sayings (the hypothetical Q document) which Mt and Lk employed independently of each other. With the exception of the gospels, there is no other New Testament writing which rings with so many echoes of Jesus' sayings as does Jas.

There are two features of the Epistle of James which are distinctly christian: 1) the eschatological motivation which undergirds its moral exhortation, and 2) the author's designation of the gospel as the "law of liberty."

Just as Jesus proclaimed the coming of God's perfect Reign and, while promising participation in the glorious Kingdom, threatened with condemnation and punishment those who refused to accept him as the agent of the coming Kingdom, so the moral exhortation of Jas contains both a positive and a negative eschatological feature. The promise of the Beatitudes is echoed again and again in the Epistle, e.g. Jas 2:5 "Listen, my beloved brethren, has not God chosen those who are poor in the world to be rich in faith and heirs of the Kingdom which he has promised to those who love him?" And like Jesus (and Paul too), James buttresses his call to repentance with the threat of condemnation at the final judgment. (cmp. Mt 12:36-37 and Jas 3:1-12; Mt 5:7 and Jas 2:13; also Rom 14:4 and Jas 4:11-12).

James shares the belief, which is central in New Testament eschatology, that "the age to come" (to use Paul's rabbinical term) dawned with the Lord's resurrection and that the present time constitutes "the last days." At any moment the Risen Lord may come back: "the *Parousia* of the Lord is at hand," "behold the judge is standing at the doors" (Jas 5:7-9). Consequently an exhortation to patient endurance, to steadfastness in the midst of trials is a prominent feature of Jas just as it is of the Jesus' Sayings of the gospels (cf. esp. Mk 13 and the parallel passages of Lk and Mt), of Paul's epistles, of the Book of Revelation – indeed of the whole New Testament. So the ethics of Jas, like that of Jesus, is an interim ethics, understanding the phrase in its true New Testament meaning, namely a moral teaching for this final period of salvation history which dawned with the coming of Jesus and his death and resurrection and perdures until the end of history at his glorious *Parousia*.

The statement frequently made by commentators of Jas that the Epistle contains no Christian theology needs a radical modification. If New Testament theology is identified exclusively with Christology, then Jas does not contain theology. But if eschatology is an integral part of New Testament theology and, indeed, of New Testament Christology, then the Epistle of James is a distinguished representative of New Testament ethical, or moral, theology. Franz Mussner declares that "it is precisely the eschatology which gives James' Epistle its distinct physiognomy and makes it essentially more than a mere collection of traditional hortatory wisdom maxims."

THE GREETING.
1:1.

> **1** James, a servant of God and of the Lord Jesus Christ,
> To the twelve tribes in the Dispersion: Greeting.

The quality of the Greek, both as regards vocabulary and rhetoric, makes very improbable the traditional opinion that the actual author of the Epistle was James, the Lord's brother, whom St. Jerome identified with the Apostle

James of Alphaeus. As late as 1964 Franz Mussner, the German Catholic exegete, who has written an excellent commentary on the Epistle, still maintained that the author was James, the Lord's brother. But he rejected the identification of this James with the apostle, James of Alphaeus. The New Testament makes it quite clear that none of Jesus' brethren belonged to the company of the twelve apostles. Acts 1:13-14 after listing the Apostles by name, continues "together they (i.e. the Apostles) devoted themselves to constant prayer. There were some women in their company, and Mary, the mother of the Lord, and his brothers." The lists of the Apostles in Mk, Mt and Lk do not mention any brother of the Lord (cf. Mk 3:14-19; Mt 10:1-4; Lk 6:12-16). Moreover the Apostles had already been chosen when Jesus' brethren still refused to believe him. Mk 3:20-22 implies that the brothers of Jesus were opposed to his ministry. Jn 7:5 expressly notes that the brothers of the Lord did not believe him. Acts 1:14 would seem to indicate that it was the Lord's resurrection which led the brothers to believe. (1 Cor 15:7 mentions an apparition of the Risen Lord to James, the Lord's brother.) The identification of James, the Lord's brother, with the apostle James of Alphaeus rests on the statement of Paul (Gal 1:19) that on his first trip to Jerusalem to visit Peter after his conversion he saw "none of the other Apostles, except James, the Lord's brother." But the Greek text is ambiguous. The particle *ei me* frequently means "except." But it has also the adversative meaning "but only." The translation "I did not see any other apostle (i.e. besides Peter) but (I saw) only James, the Lord's brother," would seem to be the meaning intended by Paul. The statement of Paul in Gal 2:9 that, on the occasion of his second visit to Jerusalem when the question of Gentile liberty from the law was debated (the so-called Council of Jerusalem of Acts 15), "those who were the acknowledged pillars, James, Cephas (i.e. Peter) and John, gave Barnabas and me the handclasp of friendship" in no way forces upon us the conclusion that James was an apostle.

His role of leader of the Jewish-Christian community of Jerusalem clearly depicted in Acts explains Paul's regard for him as a pillar of the Church.

The prevailing opinion among New Testament scholars today, Catholics and Protestants, is that Jas is a pseudonymous writing. A Jewish-Christian of the Hellenistic world presented his writing as a message to his Christian readers from James, the Lord's brother, who had been the leader of the mother Church of Jerusalem and who was martyred about 62 A.D. There is, however, a difficulty with this common opinion. If the unknown author were presenting his writing as a message from James, the Lord's brother, he should have stated this expressly. We should have expected the opening verse to read: "James a servant of God and *brother* of the Lord Jesus Christ" – just as the unknown author of the Pastoral Epistles expressly presents himself as "Paul, an Apostle of Christ Jesus" (1 Tim 1:1; Titus 1:1), and as the author of Second Peter, the last New Testament writing, introduces himself: "Simeon Peter, servant and apostle of Jesus Christ" (2 Pt 1:1). If the author of Jas wished to place his writing under the aegis of the Lord's brother, why doesn't he say so clearly?

James (Jacob) was a very common name. All that can be concluded from the Epistle itself is that a Hellenistic Christian, probably a convert from Judaism, thoroughly conversant with the hortatory literature of Judaism and the ethical teaching of Jesus, wrote this forceful exhortation to live sincerely a life according to the law of liberty, i.e. the gospel commandment of love.

This unknown James, whose mother tongue was Greek, addresses his exhortation "to the twelve tribes in the Dispersion." Are the addressees Jewish-Christian communities outside Palestine? Many have thought so; and some scholars still do. More probably, in view of the fact that, except for the opening verse, the writing has none of the usual characteristics of a letter, e.g. no allusions to the personal relationship of writer and readers – not even the customary concluding salutation – the expression "the twelve tribes of the Dispersion" is employed with the same meaning it has in 1 Pt 1:1, namely to designate Christians who are (to borrow Paul's expression in Gal 5:16) "the Israel of God" whose true homeland is heaven and who are living as pilgrims and strangers in an unbelieving and hostile world.

Those who hold that James, the Lord's brother, wrote the epistle date it before his death in 62-63 A.D. Some maintain that Jas is the earliest, the first New Testament writing, and they date it between 40-50 A.D. Among those who regard the epistle as pseudonymous a few scholars (e.g. A. Harnack and M. Dibelius) date it very late, in the middle of the second century A.D. Most scholars today think that Jas was written toward the end of the first century, i.e. 80-100 A.D.

Jas 3:1 translated nicely by RSV: "Let not many of you become teachers, my brethren, for you know that we who teach shall be judged with greater strictness" tells us that the author had received the charism of teaching and exercised that ministry in his church (cf. 1 Cor 12:28; Rom 12:7). The polemic against those who hold that faith alone justifies and that there is no obligation for believers to perform virtuous deeds, and the author's conclusion from the example of Abraham contrary to Paul's conclusion from the same Patriarch's history (Rom 4), quite clearly indicate that James opposes teachers who were promoting a moral permissiveness, a libertinism, because of their distorted interpretation of Paul's teaching on gratuitous justification.

The author (a Christian teacher called James) and his readers (Christian communities comprising converts from Judaism and paganism) lived in the Hellenistic world. Syria, Asia Minor, Egypt, even Rome have been suggested. We simply do not know and all attempts to locate "the twelve tribes in the Dispersion" of 1:1 are pure conjectures.

SUFFERING AND PRAYER.
1:2-8.

> [2] Count it all joy, my brethren, when you meet various trials, [3] for you know that the testing of your faith produces steadfastness. [4] And let steadfastness have its full effect, that you may be perfect and complete, lacking in nothing.
>
> [5] If any of you lacks wisdom, let him ask God, who gives to all men generously and without reproaching, and it will be given him. [6] But let him ask in faith, with no doubting, for he who doubts is like a wave of the sea that is driven and tossed by the wind. [7,8] For that person must not suppose that a double-minded man, unstable in all his ways, will receive anything from the Lord.

A characteristic feature of Jas is the author's use of catchwords to link together his moral maxims. For example: the word *hypomonē* (steadfastness or patient endurance) links together verses 3 and 4; "the testing of your faith produces steadfastness. And let steadfastness have its full effect (lit. "perfect work") that you may be perfect."

Jas employs the vocabulary of New Testament eschatological teaching: trials (*peirasmoi*), steadfastness or patience (*hypomonē*). For Christians the present time is the "last days." Believing Christians hope for and await the *parousia*, the coming of their Risen Lord, to usher in the glorious reign of God which will be the perfect completion of the Redemption accomplished in the Lord's death and resurrection. The call to discipleship is an invitation to follow Jesus on the way of the cross (Mk 8:31-35; 1 Pt 2:21). Suffering is a condition for growth in the Christian life; through trials the disciples progress toward full participation in the Lord's resurrected life (cf. Acts 14:21-22; Rom 8:16-18; 1 Pt 1:7; 4:3). Consequently, the exhortation to steadfastness in faith, to patient endurance, is a constant theme of New Testament eschatology (cf. e.g. Lk 21:12-19;

Acts 14:21-22; Rom 8:16-18). Joy in suffering is the astounding paradox of Christian existence because of faith in Jesus' Resurrection. James' invitation "Count it all joy when you meet various trials" expresses a common New Testament theme (cf. Mt 5:11-12; Acts 5:40-41; Col 1:24; 1 Pt 4:13). Like Paul, James views trials as a test which will show the sincerity and steadfastness of one's faith (Rom 5:3-5).

The Beatitudes, which hail as fortunate the poor, the hungry, the sorrowing, the despised and persecuted (Lk 6:20-22), are utter foolishness to a purely natural, rational evaluation of human happiness. The New Testament paradox of joy in suffering is, like the good news of redemption through Christ crucified, a scandal and an absurdity to those who do not have Christian faith, who judge by a worldly wisdom (1 Cor 1:18-25; 3:19), a wisdom which James calls "earthly, unspiritual, devilish" (Jas 3:15).

Even for the believing Christian the experience of trials, pain, sufferings may become a scandal, a temptation to question the loving Providence of God. True wisdom is God's gift to us in Christ through the Spirit. James exhorts the tempted Christian to pray to God who always "gives generously and without reproaching." But prayer must proceed from faith, i.e. from an unwavering filial confidence in God's goodness and love. We are reminded of Jesus' teaching in the Sermon on the Mount (Mt 7:7-12) and especially of Luke's expression of it: "For everyone who asks receives, and he who seeks finds, and to him who knocks, it will be opened . . . If you then who are evil, know how to give good gifts to your children, how much more will the heavenly Father give the Holy Spirit to those who ask him!" (Lk 11:10-13).

A CHRISTIAN EVALUATION OF LIFE.
1:9-12.

> 9Let the lowly brother boast in his exaltation, 10and the rich in his humiliation, because like the flower of

the grass he will pass away. ¹¹For the sun rises with its scorching heat and withers the grass; its flower falls, and its beauty perishes. So will the rich man fade away in the midst of his pursuits.

¹²Blessed is the man who endures trial, for when he has stood the test he will receive the crown of life which God has promised to those who love him.

Enlightened by the wisdom from above, the faithful, both poor and rich, will evaluate their lives by God's measure and not by the world's. The rich Christian will be keenly aware of his mortality and will be preserved through his belief in the judgment of God and the eschatological goal of human existence from a false sense of security in his possessions. Jas exhorts him to boast in his humiliation, in the knowledge that he can't take it with him. James borrows the vivid metaphors of the Old Testament to express this truth, e.g. Ps 103:15-16 "As for man his days are like grass; he flourishes like a flower of the field; for the wind passes over it, and it is gone, and its place knows it no more"; Is 40:6-7 "All flesh is grass, and all its beauty is like the flower of the field, the grass withers, the flower fades."

The lowly, poor Christian, who through the gift of wisdom knows God's predilection for the humble and afflicted, should exult in the exaltation which awaits him in the glorious Kingdom of God. So James concludes his contrast of the poor and the rich with a Beatitude (v.12) reminiscent of Jesus' Beatitudes (Mt 5:10-12) and of the Risen Lord's promise through the prophet John to the suffering Christians of Smyrna (Rev 2:10).

THE ORIGIN OF TEMPTATIONS.
1:13-18.

¹³Let no one say when he is tempted, "I am tempted by God"; for God cannot be tempted with evil and he

himself tempts no one; [14]but each person is tempted when he is lured and enticed by his own desire. [15]Then desire when it has conceived gives birth to sin; and sin when it is full-grown brings forth death.

[16]Do not be deceived, my beloved brethren. [17]Every good endowment and every perfect gift is from above, coming down from the Father of lights with whom there is no variation or shadow due to change. [18]Of his own will he brought us forth by the word of truth that we should be a kind of first fruits of his creatures.

James distinguishes between trials and temptations to sin. God, who is infinitely good and holy, tempts no one to sin. He is the source of every good endowment of nature and of grace. He is immutable in his holiness and goodness. This truth is expressed by the biblical metaphor which contrasts good and evil as light and darkness, God is "the Father of lights" i.e. the creator of sun, moon and stars. Unlike these created heavenly lights which are subject to variations in their positions (the Greek word employed by Jas probably refers to the parallax of the sun and stars) and are darkened by the shadows of eclipses, God's light (his goodness and holiness) is always the same, infinitely perfect. With the Father of lights there is absolutely undimmed and continuous splendor.

Temptation to sin has its source in selfish desire. Jas pictures this desire as a prostitute. Consent to the seduction gives birth to sin, and sin brings forth death which, in the context, can only mean the loss of the new life which is God's gift in Christ (cf. "The crown of life" v.12 and birth from God v.18).

Verse 18 is an explicit antithesis to verse 15. The verb "to bring forth" (*apokuein*) occurs nowhere else in the New Testament. It describes the action of a woman bringing forth a child from her womb. Jas uses this "feminine" verb of God instead of the "masculine" verb "to beget" (*gennan*) employed by other New Testament writers, because he wishes to draw a parallel, an antithetical parallel, with verse 15. "Sin when it is full-grown brings forth death"(15). God "brought us forth by the word of truth" (18).

James' teaching on spiritual birth from God (v.18): "Of his own will he brought us forth by the word of truth that we should be a kind of first fruits of his creation" expresses the divine initiative in the justification and salvation of mankind as clearly as do Paul, 1 Pt and 1 Jn. In placing the participle *boulētheis* "Of his own free will," at the beginning of the sentence James is emphasizing it. He is stressing the freedom of God's will and action. Philo uses this Greek participle to express the sovereign liberty of God in creating the universe. James employs it to express the free, sovereign creative will and action of God in "the new creation," the redemption of mankind and the world (cf. also Heb 6:17; 2 Pt 3:9 for a similar use of this verb). It is "by the word of truth" that God brings forth his children of the new creation. In the New Testament, with the exception of Jas, the expression "word of truth" occurs only in the Pauline writings where it refers to the proclamation of the gospel. Paul tells the Corinthians that he and his fellow missionaries always strive to present themselves as sincere ministers of God, as men "with a word of truth and a power of God" (2 Cor 6:7). We are reminded of the Apostle's description of the preaching of the gospel as a power of God for salvation to everyone who believes (Rom 1:16). Col 1:5 and Eph 1:13 expressly equate "the word of truth" with "the gospel."

James description of the goal of our birth from God, "that we should be a kind of first fruits of his creatures," is very similar to Paul's teaching: "If anyone is in Christ he is a new creation" (2 Cor 5:17). In the Old Testament "first fruit" is a technical liturgical term. "All that first opens the womb" of women and animals, i.e. the firstborn son and the firstborn male animals, belong to the Lord and must be redeemed, i.e. bought back by an offering of sacrifice (cf. Ex 13:11-13). The first fruit of the harvest must also be offered to the Lord (cf. Ex 23:19; Dt 26:1-11). Through these offerings Israel recognized her redemption from Egyptian bondage, Israel redeemed from slavery was herself "holy to the Lord, the first fruits of his harvest" (Jer 2:3). The New Testament also employs this term to signify the divine election of Christians. In the Book of Revelation (14:4) the 144,000 who have remained faithful in spite of persecution, who stand on Mt. Zion with the Lamb and sing a new song in the liturgy being celebrated before God's throne, are those who have been redeemed as first fruits for God and the Lamb. In 1 Cor 15:20 the Risen Christ is called the first fruit of those who have died. In both these passages (Rev and 1 Cor) the eschatological dimension of the term "first fruit" is prominent. This is also true of James' use of the term. Through the preaching of the gospel, the word of truth, God by his own free creative action has made Christians his children in order that they might be the first fruit of his new creation, the eschatological creation. Franz Mussner (*op. cit.*) thinks that James' use of first fruits in 1:18 probably echoes the baptismal liturgy of his community. He points to a similar baptismal text in 1 Pt 1:23,25: "You have been born anew, not of perishable seed but of imperishable, through the living and abiding word of God . . . That word is the good news which was preached to you."

GENUINE PIETY AND TRUE RELIGION.
1:19-27.

19 Know this, my beloved brethren. Let every man be quick to hear, slow to speak, slow to anger, 20 for the anger of man does not work the righteousness of God. 21 Therefore put away all filthiness and rank growth of wickedness and receive with meekness the implanted word, which is able to save your souls.

22 But be doers of the word, and not hearers only, deceiving yourselves. 23 For if any one is a hearer of the

word and not a doer, he is like a man who observes his natural face in a mirror; 24for he observes himself and goes away and at once forgets what he was like. 25But he who looks into the perfect law, the law of liberty, and perseveres, being no hearer that forgets but a doer that acts, he shall be blessed in his doing.

26If any one thinks he is religious, and does not bridle his tongue but deceives his heart, this man's religion is vain. 27Religion that is pure and undefiled before God and the Father is this: to visit the orphans and widows in their affliction, and to keep oneself unstained from the world.

This series of maxims stresses the pastoral concern of Jas: a practical Christianity. Christians must live according to the gospel which they have accepted in faith. The exhortation to be quick to hear, slow to speak, slow to anger is a traditional biblical teaching on the conditions necessary for a peaceful society (cf. James' favorite Old Testament book Sir 5:11-14, the Sermon on the Mount Mt 5:22; also Col 3:8-9; Eph 4:25-31). Patient listening helps one to avoid quick responses that may lead to an angry outburst. Anger does not work the righteousness of God, i.e. it does not promote the peace and harmony which is the fruit of the observance of God's commandment of love of the neighbor (cf. Ps 15:1-3). Does Jas have in mind here "the wars and fightings among you" of which he speaks in 4:1? He probably is thinking of the quarrels and disputes which were destroying the peace of the Christian communities to which he sent his letter, but his exhortation is as pertinent and timely today as it was in the closing years of the first century A.D.

"The implanted word, which is able to save your souls," is the gospel. It was through the proclamation of this "word of truth" (1:18) that believers became, through God's grace, his children, his chosen people. Perhaps Jas has in mind Jeremiah's description of the new covenant: "I will put my law within them, and I will write it upon their hearts"

(Jer 31:33). Since the word is implanted by God James' exhortation to receive it with meekness cannot refer to the initial act of faith responding to God's call and action. It is rather, as the context clearly shows, an exhortation to live according to the gospel, i.e. to put away, as one casts off dirty clothing, every tendency of self-centered egoism and of past self-indulgence which would keep one from following Jesus, who was meek and humble of heart (cf. Eph 4:25-31; Col 3:8-10). Paul frequently uses the verb "put on" or "clothe yourselves with" as the antithesis of the verb "to put away," "to strip or cast off" e.g. Rom 13:12-14: "Let us then cast off the works of darkness and put on the armor of light; let us conduct ourselves becomingly . . . not in reveling and drunkenness, not in debauchery and licentiousness, not in quarreling and jealousy. But put on the Lord Jesus Christ." James employs "receive" as the antithesis to "put away."

The power to bring us to salvation belongs to the implanted word. This teaching of James is of capital importance for a balanced assessment of his theology on the relation of works to faith. He attributes salvation to the gospel. His statement is very similar to Paul's declaration that the gospel is "the power of God for salvation to everyone who has faith" (Rom 1:16). Like James, Paul, in all his epistles, exhorts his readers to live according to the gospel.

Verses 22-25 echo the conclusion of the Sermon on the Mount (Mt 7:24-27). They are a warning against self-deception and hypocrisy. God has redeemed us in Jesus Crucified and Risen. His merciful goodness, love and saving power are active in the preaching of the gospel. Our response in faith to God's saving action is also due to his grace. "No one" Christ declared "can come to me unless the Father who sent me draws him" (Jn 6:4). "For by grace you have been saved through faith; and this is not your own doing, it is the gift of God"(Eph 2:8). This gracious gift of God by which we became brothers and sisters of Christ imposes on us the obligation of cooperating with the Spirit dwelling within us. We must live according to the gospel so that through our deeds the world may come to recognize the presence of Christ the Savior in his church. The Epistle to the Ephesians expresses nicely this teaching which is the very heart of James' exhortation: "For we are his (God's) workmanship, created in Christ Jesus for good works, which God prepared beforehand, that we should walk in them" (Eph 2:10). A person who believes that the gospel is true, but does not live according to it, is like a man who looks at himself in a mirror and then forgets what he has seen. The pagan writer Seneca also employed this example to teach a moral lesson. He tells us that mirrors were invented so that people might see the physical blemishes and defects which they should try to correct. A person with physical blemishes, he goes on to say, can make up for the lack of physical beauty by the practice of virtue. In James' use of the example the mirror is the gospel, its ethical demands as well as its doctrinal teaching. The mirror of the gospel reveals to the Christian the sins and faults that are impeding his transformation into the likeness of Christ, his Lord. The "hearer only of the word" does nothing to emend his life. But the person who has bent over to look carefully into the gospel and who perseveres in the observance of its ethical demands, is a doer of the word "who shall be blessed in his doing."

The perfect law of liberty is "the implanted word," i.e. the gospel. The core of this perfect law is for James Jesus' interpretation of love of the neighbor (cf. 2:8; Mt 22:39; 25:40,45). For James the gospel is law. But it is the perfect law of liberty because it frees the Christian who follows Jesus' example and teaching of self-emptying love and service for others from the shackles of selfish egoism which is the source of all the evils which destroy the peace of society and impede the Christian's growth in holiness.

The conclusion of this section of the epistle recapitulates the opening verses (19-21). Genuine piety is recognized by disciplined speech (19-20), and true religion by concern for the needs of the poor and afflicted and by repudiation of the vices of the world, i.e. of worldlings who make pleasure and self-satisfaction their life's goal. James echoes the teaching of the prophets (e.g. Is 1:10-27; Amos 5:21-26) illustrated so graphically and emphatically by Jesus in his description of the last judgment, Mt 25:31-46. "I was hungry and you gave me food . . . naked and you clothed me . . . Truly, I say to you, as you did it to one of the least of these my brethren, you did it to me" (cf. also 1 Jn 3:23; 4:20-21; 2:15-17).

FAVORITISM AND THE COMING JUDGMENT. 2:1-13.

2 My brethren, show no partiality as you hold the faith of our Lord Jesus Christ, the Lord of glory. ²For if a man with gold rings and in fine clothing comes into your assembly, and a poor man in shabby clothing also comes in, ³and you pay attention to the one who wears the fine clothing and say, "Have a seat here, please," while you say to the poor man, "Stand there," or, "Sit at my feet," ⁴have you not made distinctions among yourselves, and become judges with evil thoughts? ⁵Listen, my beloved brethren. Has not God chosen those who are poor in the world to be rich in faith and heirs of the kingdom which he has promised to those who love him? ⁶But you have dishonored the poor man. Is it not the rich who oppress you, is it not they who drag you into court? ⁷Is it not they who blaspheme the honorable name which was invoked over you?

⁸If you really fulfil the royal law, according to the scripture, "You shall love your neighbor as yourself, " you do well. ⁹But if you show partiality, you commit sin, and are convicted by the law as transgressors. ¹⁰For whoever keeps the whole law but fails in one point has become guilty of all of it. ¹¹For he who said, "Do not commit adultery," said also, "Do not kill." If you do not

commit adultery but do kill, you have become a trans-
gressor of the law. [12]So speak and so act as those who
are to be judged under the law of liberty. [13]For judgment
is without mercy to one who has shown no mercy; yet
mercy triumphs over judgment.

James now turns to a new theme which he presents as
intimately associated with his teaching on true religion.
Discrimination against the poor and partiality toward
the rich, special marks of esteem given solely because of
wealth and social status, are incompatible with faith in
Jesus Christ the glorious Lord. The Christian believes
that Jesus the Risen Lord of glory is he who emptied himself
through death on the cross, he who voluntarily chose
poverty and humiliation so that by his poverty and shameful
death we might be redeemed and share in the riches and
glory of God's Kingdom (cf. Phil 2:5-11; 2 Cor 8:9). The
Christian must evaluate everyone and everything by the
gospel. The phrase "Jesus Christ the Lord of Glory" is a
confession of Christian faith based on the early creedal
liturgical acclamation "Jesus Christ is Lord!" It proclaims
the Christian belief that Jesus of Nazareth who was crucified
is the promised Messiah (Christ) and the Lord who has been
glorified through Resurrection from the dead. The object
of Christian faith is the gospel in its entirety, the person,
mission and teaching of Jesus. To honor the rich because of
their wealth and to despise the poor because of their
poverty, is unchristian because diametrically opposed to
the gospel. Such favoritism and discrimination proceeds
from "earthly, unspiritual, devilish" wisdom (3:25) and
not from faith in Christ Crucified who is "the wisdom
of God" (1 Cor 1:24).

James gives a vivid description of an incident of favoritism
that may happen when the community assembles for worship. The conjunction "if" introduces a hypothetical example. But this may be James' tactful manner of reminding

his readers of actual cases of partiality that have occurred in the Christian assemblies (cf. v.6).

How different is God's standard of judgment from that of those who curry the favor of the wealthy and despise the poor! Both the Old and New Testaments emphasize God's special, preferential love of the *anawim*, the poor, lowly and afflicted who are truly humble. In itself poverty, like all suffering and deprivation, is evil. Wealth in itself is a good, a blessing. But from the religious viewpoint it is evident that all too frequently riches are an obstacle to faith and to the following of Christ in his complete surrender to His Father and in his self-emptying love of mankind. The sense of security which wealth brings impedes the recognition of absolute dependance on God which is the necessary disposition for the act of faith. The poor, the afflicted, the persecuted, because of the circumstances of their existence, can more easily recognize their creaturely dependance on God and so are more readily disposed to make the act of faith which is a total surrender of oneself to God in confident hope and filial love. It is easier for the poor to become poor in spirit than it is for the rich. "Truly, I say to you, it will be hard for a rich man to enter the kingdom of heaven" (Mt 19:23).

"He who mocks the poor insults his Maker" (Prov 17:5). Discrimination against the poor is an insult to God. With a rhetorical question: "has not God chosen those who are poor in the world to be rich in faith and heirs of the kingdom which he has promised to those who love him?" James reminds his readers of Jesus' promise of the Kingdom of God to the poor (Lk 6:20) and also of the low social and economic class to which the majority of Christians belong. "For consider your own call, brethren; not many of you were wise according to worldly standards, not many were powerful, not many were of noble birth; but God chose what is foolish in the world to shame the wise, God chose what is weak in the world to shame the strong, God chose what is low and despised in the world, even things that are not, to bring to nothing things that are, so that no human being might boast in the presence of God" (1 Cor 1:26-29, Paul's description of the Corinthian community). James' expression "poor in the world" refers to an economic and social condition, "Rich in faith" means rich because of faith, rather than an abundant faith. Christians are children of God, heirs of God, fellow heirs with Christ called to share in the glory of their Risen Lord. The Spirit they have received is the guarantee, indeed the first installment, the down payment of their glorious inheritance (cf. 2 Cor 1:22; 5:5; Eph 1:13-14; Rom 8:15-16).

Partiality toward the rich obsequiously honors the very social class which exploits the poor, harasses Christians, and dishonors Christ the Lord of glory. "Is it not they who blaspheme the honorable name by which you are called?" The faithful were called Christians (Acts 11:25). A literal translation of the Greek text "the good name which is invoked over you" is a biblical expression which designates the chosen people of God (e.g. Dt 28:10; Amos 9:12; Jer 6:10). Christians are "the Israel of God" (Gal 6:16), chosen in Christ Jesus. In a passage that is a mosaic of phrases from the Old Testament especially the Prophets, James (5:4-6) gives a graphic description of the exploitation and persecution which the poor suffer at the hands of the rich.

Verses 8-13; verse 8 is a conditional sentence. Perhaps James had in mind an objection which some of his readers might raise against his condemnation of partiality toward the rich. They might say: "In giving marks of respect and esteem to the wealthy we are observing the law of love for the neighbor." James' conditional sentence implies that proper respect for persons of authority, leadership and influence in society and in the Christian communities is good and laudable. But, not if it is accompanied by discrimination against the poor and motivated solely because of wealth. He calls the law of love of the neighbor promulgated in the book of Leviticus (19:18) the royal law. "The law of liberty" in verse 12 is the gospel (cf. Jas 1:25). The royal law refers, therefore, to the gospel interpretation of love for the neighbor. Some commentators think James calls love for the neighbor "the royal law" because it was given a new interpretation by Christ, the King, or because the kingdom of heaven is promised to those who observe it (cf. Mt 25:31-40). More probably "royal" means simply first among all the commandments. Jesus declared that "all the law and the prophets" depend on the double commandment of love of God and love of the neighbor (Mt 22:36-40). While love of God is "the great and first commandment" it is indissolubly linked to love of the neighbor. Indeed sincere love of God is impossible without love of the neighbor (cf. 1 Jn 3:14-18; 4:20-21). Perhaps with Prov 14:21 in mind: "He who despises his neighbor is a sinner, but happy is he who is kind to the poor." James declares that those who show partiality are sinners. In fact because all God's moral precepts are expressions of the law of love, they are guilty of the entire law. This is also the teaching of Paul in Rom 13:8-10. James chooses the commandments forbidding murder and adultery to illustrate his teaching. His favorite Old Testament book describes exploitation of the poor and refusal to help the needy as murder (Sir 34:20-22), and for James currying the favor of the rich is a kind of spiritual adultery.

This section concludes with a reminder of the final judgment. The criterion by which we shall be judged is "the law of liberty," the gospel commandment of love. Verse 13 echoes the beatitude: "Blessed are the merciful, for they shall obtain mercy" (Mt 5:7).

FAITH WITHOUT WORKS IS DEAD.
2:14-26.

> [14]What does it profit, my brethren, if a man says he has faith but has not works? Can his faith save him? [15]If a brother or sister is ill-clad and in lack of daily food, [16]and

one of you says to them, "Go in peace, be warmed and filled," without giving them the things needed for the body, what does it profit? [17]So faith by itself, if it has no works, is dead.

[18]But someone will say, "You have faith and I have works." Show me your faith apart from your works, and I by my works will show you my faith. [19]You believe that God is one; you do well. Even the demons believe – and shudder. [20]Do you want to be shown, you shallow man, that faith apart from works is barren? [21]Was not Abraham our Father justified by works, when he offered his son Isaac upon the altar? [22]You see that faith was active along with his works, and faith was completed by works, [23]and the scripture was fulfilled which says, "Abraham believed God, and it was reckoned to him as righteousness"; and he was called the friend of God. [24]You see that a man is justified by works and not by faith alone. [25]And in the same way was not also Rahab the harlot justified by works when she received the messengers and sent them out another way? [26]For as the body apart from the spirit is dead, so faith apart from works is dead.

James insists with ever increasing urgency on the necessity of a living practical Christianity. He knows that Christianity is rooted in faith. He has spoken of faith in 1:3 and 2:1. In chapter one he contrasted the doers of the word to the hearers only. Now he contrasts "faith only" with a faith that manifests itself in deeds. Employing the Greek rhetorical device called diatribe, he engages in a lively discussion with an imaginary opponent and concludes with the emphatic declaration that "faith by itself is dead" (v.17), as useless for salvation as the faith of the demons who acknowledge the unity of God but none the less shudder with fear (v.19). Faith is an acknowledgment and profession of the truth that God the omnipotent and loving creator has revealed his mercy and love and restored sinful humanity to

a living filial union with himself in Christ Jesus our Lord
(1:18). This faith is the heart and core of Christianity.
But, and this is the thesis of the epistle, the believer's
response to God's gracious gift of faith demands that he
show his love for God his Father by following Jesus in his
unselfish love of mankind (1:27). The believer whose faith
is not expressed in deeds of love for the neighbor is like a
person who dismisses the hungry and the naked with a
hypocritical wish that their suffering be alleviated but does
not move a finger to help them. Such a believer is a pious
fraud. Two biblical examples illustrate the thesis that true,
sincere faith is completed and perfected by deeds. The
first is an incident from the story of Abraham, the father
of Israel and our "Father in Faith" (Gal 3:29; Rom 4:1,12).
"Was not Abraham our Father justified by works, when he
offered his son Isaac upon the altar? (Gen 22) You see that
faith was active along with his works, and faith was completed by works, and the scripture was fulfilled (Gen 15:6)
which says 'Abraham believed God, and it was reckoned to
him as righteousness' and he was called the friend of God"
(verses 21-23). This example was probably suggested to
James by Sir 44:19-20 and 1 Mac 2:52. Both see the proof
of Abraham's faith in his testing, namely his readiness to
obey God's command that he sacrifice Isaac, the son of
promise. Like 1 Mac, James applies to Abraham's readiness
to sacrifice Isaac the praise given by Gen 15:6 to the Patriarch's faith in God's promise that he would father a son of
Isaac and be the progenitor of a numerous nation. The
Epistle to the Hebrews also appeals to Gen 22 as a proof
of Abraham's sincere faith: "By faith Abraham, when he
was tested, offered up Isaac, and he who had received
the promises was ready to offer up his only son, of whom
it was said, 'Through Isaac shall your descendants be
named'" (Heb 11:17-18).

The second biblical example James adduces in support
of his thesis is the story of Rahab, the harlot of Jericho,
(Jos 2:1-21). Because she believed that God had given the

city of Jericho and the land to the Israelites, she saved, at the risk of her own life, the lives of the two spies sent by Joshua. In return she and all her family were saved when the Israelites conquered Jericho. The early church held Rahab in high esteem. She is listed among the ancestors of Jesus (Mt 1:5) and, like Jas, the epistle to the Hebrews (Heb 11:31) and the first Epistle of Clement of Rome (1 Clement 12) hail her as an example of faith which proves itself by deeds.

James and Paul

Is there a contradiction between James' teaching on the necessity of good works for justification and Paul's teaching on justification by faith apart from works? Luther maintained that James "is flatly against St. Paul and all the rest of Scripture in ascribing justification to works." (Preface to the Epistles of St. James and St. Jude). The key texts are Jas 2:24 and Rom 3:28. James declares "You see that a man is justified by works and not by faith alone"; while Paul teaches: "For we hold that a man is justified by faith apart from works of law."

Both James and Paul appeal to the example of Abraham and cite the same Old Testament text, Gen 15:6, in support of their theses. James sees Abraham's readiness to obey God's command that he sacrifice Isaac as proof of his thesis. Paul points to Abraham's faith in God's promise that he would have a son by Sarah (Gn 15:1-6; 12:1-3). He writes in Rom 4:2-5: "For if Abraham was justified by works, he has something to boast about, but not before God. For what does the scripture say? 'Abraham believed God, and it was reckoned to him as righteousness.' Now to one who works, his wages are not reckoned as a gift but as his due. And to one who does not work but trusts him who justifies the ungodly, his faith is reckoned as righteousness." And the Apostle concludes (Rom 4:23-25): "But the words, 'it was reckoned to him,' were written not for his sake alone, but for ours also. It will be reckoned to us who believe in him that raised from the dead Jesus our Lord, who was put to death for our trespasses and raised for our justification."

James' use of Gen 15:6 in support of his thesis is strong evidence that he is challenging the Pauline slogan "faith apart from works." But an analysis of the diverse meanings which Paul and James attach to the terms faith, works, justification in their theses, and especially Paul's exhortations to live according to the Spirit and not according to the flesh, to follow Christ's example of humble love and service, which are an integral part of every Pauline letter, support the conclusion that James had never read the Apostle's epistles (cf. e.g. Gal 5:13-6:10; Rom 8:12-13; 14:10-13; Phil 2:1-13).

James is opposing the use of the Pauline slogan by false teachers who were promoting a moral permissiveness on the basis of the apostle's thesis of justification by faith. Second and third century gnostics interpreted Paul's epistles as a permission for moral license. They turned Christian liberty into libertinism. The last writing of the New Testament, the Second Epistle of Peter, composed between 120-150 A.D. refers to this abuse of Paul's epistles which were then regarded as sacred scripture. "There are some things in them hard to understand, which the ignorant and unstable twist to their own destruction, as they do the other scriptures. You therefore, beloved, knowing this beforehand, beware lest you are carried away with the error of lawless men and lose your own stability" (2 Pt 3:15-17).

Even during his own lifetime Paul was misunderstood and his teaching on Christian liberty distorted and abused. In the very epistles in which he expounds his teaching on gratuitous justification by faith he warns against confusing Christian freedom from the Law with moral permissiveness. "For you were called to freedom, brethren; only do not use your freedom as an opportunity for the flesh, but through love be servants of one another. For the whole law is fulfilled in one word, "you shall love your neighbor as yourself" (Gal 5:13-14). Rom 3:8 "And why not do evil that good may come? – as some people slanderously charge us with saying. Their condemnation is just" implies that some misunderstood, and even distorted his teaching on redemption and justification (cf. also Rom 6:1-2, 12-15).

Faith in the Pauline letters, especially in Romans, usually signifies man's surrender to God's saving love, power and action present in the proclamation of the gospel which reveals the divine redemption of the world in Jesus Crucified and Risen. When the hearer of the gospel makes this act of faith his sins are forgiven, he receives the life of grace, he is put right with God; i.e. he is justified (cf. Rom 1:16-17). Paul insists that this faith response is itself a favor, a gift of God. He reminds the Corinthians that their faith rests not on his persuasive preaching nor on human wisdom, but on the power on God (1 Cor 2:1-5). Pauline faith includes what traditional theology calls the virtues of faith, hope and charity.The believer assents to the truth of the gospel; he trusts in God's love and power; he is ready to obey God's will. Occasionally in Paul's writings faith designates profession of the christian creed and membership in the church, indeed Christianity itself (cf. e.g. Rom 14:1, 22,23; Gal 1:23).

Faith in James usually means belief in the truth of the gospel, i.e. the profession of the Christian creed and membership in the church (cf. e.g. 1:3). In 1:6 and 5:15 faith associated with prayer has the specific meaning of trust, of confident hope in the loving goodness and power of God. But, as Martin Dibelius notes in his excellent analysis of the meaning of faith in James: "it is only the combination with 'prayer' which achieves this meaning – therefore this meaning cannot be generalized and traced throughout all of Jas." And he concludes: "But in all the instances which have been examined thus far what is involved is the faith which the Christian has, never the faith of the sinner which first brings him to God" (*op. cit.* p. 178).

James insists that the profession of Christian faith must manifest its sincerity and vitality by hope in God and by deeds of love for the neighbor. This faith teaching is an essential element of Jesus' teaching (cf. Mk 2:5; 5:34; 9:23; 10:52) and especially Mt 7:21: "Not everyone who says to me, 'Lord, Lord,' shall enter the kingdom of heaven, but he who does the will of my Father who is in heaven."

The term "works" or "deeds" (Greek: *erga*) occurs frequently in Paul's letters. In Galatians and Romans, the epistle in which Paul expounds his thesis of justification by faith apart from works, the term has the specific meaning "works of the Jewish law." Some have seized on the expression "works of the law" in Gal and Rom as the key to solving the problem presented by Jas. "The debate, central to the history of Christianity has usually overlooked the simple fact that Paul speaks about works of the Law and does so with reference to those works that divide Jews and Gentiles, e.g. circumcision and food laws. James, on the other hand, refers to works of mercy. Thus the two statements are not only reconcilable but address themselves to quite distinct and different issues." (K. Stendahl and E. Sanders, *art. cit. Encycl. Brit.*) This is too facile a solution. Paul's thesis of Justification by faith implies that no works, nothing that a person does or can do, merits justification. "Righteousness" is God's gift to those who heed his call in the proclamation of the gospel and believe. The author of Ephesians, who has given us an excellent synthesis of Paul's theology, tells his gentile Christian readers: "For by grace you have been saved through faith; and this is not your own doing, it is the gift of God – not because of works, lest any man should boast. For we are his workmanship, created in Christ Jesus for good works, which God prepared beforehand, that we should walk in them" (Eph 2:8-10). Paul teaches that justified by faith through God's grace the believer will arrive at the goal of Christian existence, eternal salvation, if his/her "faith works through love" (Gal 5:6); if he/she cooperates with the indwelling Spirit and lives a truly Christian life. "For we must all appear before the judgment seat of Christ, so that each one may receive good or evil according to what he has done in the body" (2 Cor 5:10; also Rom 2:16; 14:10).

James uses the term "works" twelve times, in every case he is speaking of deeds of love of the neighbor. He never mentions Jewish observances. His exhortation to show the sincerity of one's faith by works of love and mercy is the exhortation of Jesus in the Sermon on the Mount: "Let your light shine before men, that they may see your good works and give glory to your Father who is in heaven" (Mt 5:16).

Justification (or righteousness) has two meanings in the Pauline letters. First, it signifies the justice, the righteousness which God has shown, namely his gracious love and mercy manifested in the redemptive death and resurrection of Christ and in the proclamation of the gospel (cf. e.g. Rom 1:17; 3:5,21,22,25,26; 10:3). Secondly, it signifies the righteousness i.e. the forgiveness of sins and the new life in Christ given to every one who on hearing the gospel surrenders to God in faith (cf. e.g. Rom 1:16; Gal 3:22). Faith, in Paul's thesis on justification, refers to this initial act of faith which is usually expressed by the reception of baptism (cf. 1 Cor 6:11). Justification in this use of the term signifies what traditional theology calls the initial gift of sanctifying grace.

In the Epistle of James, justification has the meaning common in the Old Testament and in Judaism, namely the divine declaration at the judgment that a person has lived a good life and consequently is righteous and worthy of eternal salvation. "James, when speaking of the justification, had in mind the last judgment" (J. Jeremias, "James and Paul," *The Expository Times*, 66, 1954/55, pp. 368-371).

James teaches that the Christian is by God's free choice and favor a child of God sharing the life of the new creation (1:18). There is in Jas the same tension as in Paul's epistles between the present possession of the life of grace and the future final salvation. But the final salvation is much more prominent in Jas. For James, as for Paul, there is no self-redemption. God gives "the crown of life" (4:5-6); God chooses the poor to be the heirs of his riches (2:5); God hears and exalts the humble. The saving new-creative action of God is present in the proclamation of the gospel (1:18,21; cf. Rom 1:17). James does not oppose works to faith. He insists that faith show its sincerity in deeds of love. A faith that fails "to work through love" (Paul's expression Gal 5:6) is, James declares, barren and dead. Such a faith will not receive the King's judgment: "Come, O blessed of my father, inherit the kingdom prepared for you from the foundation of the world; for I was hungry and you gave me food, I was thirsty and you gave me drink . . ." (Mt 25:34). "Truly I say to you, as you did it to one of the least of these my brothers, you did it to me" (Mt 25:40).

The great doctor of grace, St. Augustine, rightly understood both Paul and James. He wrote in his treatise on Grace and Free Will: "But some people not understanding the words of the Apostle (Paul), 'for we hold that a man is justified by faith apart from works of law,' concluded that he meant it suffices for a person to have faith even though he live badly and does not have good deeds. But this is contrary to the meaning of the Vessel of Election (Paul) who also said in a certain place: 'For in Christ Jesus neither circumcision nor uncircumcision is of any avail, but faith working through love.' This is the faith which distinguishes the faithful of God from the unclean demons: – for they also, as the apostle James says, 'believe and tremble with fear'; but they do not perform good deeds. Therefore, they do not have that faith by which the just man lives, i.e. which works through love, so that God may confer on him eternal life according to his deeds." Following Augustine, St. Thomas Aquinas solves the apparent contradiction between Rom 3:28 and Jas 2:14-16 by the distinction between works before and works after justification, understanding the term justification in its Pauline meaning (*Comm. on Rom.* 3:28).

SINS OF THE TONGUE.
A WARNING TO TEACHERS.
3:1-12.

3 Let not many of you become teachers, my brethren, for you know that we who teach shall be judged with greater strictness, [2]For we all make many mistakes, and if anyone makes no mistakes in what he says he is a perfect man, able to bridle the whole body also. [3]If we put bits into the mouths of horses that they may obey us, we guide their whole bodies. [4]Look at the ships also; though they are so great and driven by strong winds, they are guided by a very small rudder wherever the will of the pilot directs. [5]So the tongue is a little member and boasts of great things. How great a forest is set ablaze by a small fire!

[6]And the tongue is a fire. The tongue is an unrighteous world among our members, staining the whole body, setting on fire the cycle of nature, and set on fire by hell. [7]For every kind of beast and bird, of reptile and sea creature, can be tamed and has been tamed by human-kind, [8]but no human being can tame the tongue – a restless evil, full of deadly poison. [9]With it we bless the Lord and Father, and with it we curse men, who are made in the likeness of God. [10]From the same mouth come blessing and cursing. My brethren, this ought not to be so. [11]Does a spring pour forth from the same opening fresh water and brackish? [12]Can a fig tree, my brethren, yield olives, or a grapevine figs? No more can salt water yield fresh.

In 1:26 James stigmatized as vain the religion of a person who does not control his/her tongue. Now he returns to this theme and develops it by treating specifically of the danger of sinning in speech to which teachers are especially prone.

Paul enumerates teaching among the charismatic gifts which the Spirit provides for the upbuilding of the church

(1 Cor 12:28). The New Testament and early Christian literature often mention the ministry of teaching (e.g. Acts 13:1; Eph 4:11; Didache 11:1-2; 13:2). The "We" of verse 1 indicates that James places himself among those who have been called by the Spirit to the ministry of teaching. So he knows from personal experience the dangers of offending by speech to which teachers are exposed. But he probably has in mind the harm being done in some Christian communities by teachers who were influenced by the growing gnostic movement which abused Paul's teaching on Christian liberty and encouraged moral permissiveness.

James warns his readers (verses 1-2) not to ambition the ministry of teaching, because teachers will be judged with greater severity. He may be thinking of Jesus' sharp rebuke of the scribes, "they will receive a worse judgment" (Lk 20:47), and of his warning to those who sin in speech, "I tell you, on the day of judgment men will render account for every careless word they utter; for by your words you will be justified, and by your words you will be condemned" (Mt 12:36-37). Recalling some of his own shortcomings he notes that it is very difficult not to offend with the tongue, "for we all make mistakes." Perfect control of the tongue is a sign of moral perfection. A person who never offends in speech shows that he has control of all those impulses and desires which spring from pride, selfishness and sensuality. The term "body" is used because of the association of human passions and natural instincts with the body (cf. Rom 6:12-13). A man who controls his tongue is able to control himself; just as the rider who controls the horse's mouth with the bit, or the helmsman who controls the ship's rudder, guides the whole horse or ship. In spite of its small size the tongue exercises a powerful influence for good and for evil. James is thinking especially of the evil effects of intemperate and malicious speech. It "boasts of great things." Probably James has in mind the self-righteous boasting and religious snobbery of the teachers who are disturbing and perverting the Christian communities. He notes the swiftness with which the evil spreads from an insignificant beginning: "how great a forest is set ablaze by a small fire!" The tongue is "an unrighteous world among our members." This is a very literal translation of the Greek phrase *kosmos adikios*. The tongue, small though it is, can occasion so much harm that it deserves to be called a "universe of malice." With its lies and slanders, its calumnies and detractions it destroys christian community life and does irreparable harm to individuals. The tongue stains "the whole body," i.e. evil speech ruins the moral character of the speaker; "hear and understand: not what goes into the mouth defiles a man, but what comes out of the mouth, this defiles a man" (Mt 15:11). Like a little spark igniting a vast forest fire the tongue sets afire "the cycle of nature." The Greek phrase translated here "the cycle of nature" means literally "the wheel of birth" or "the wheel of being." This strange expression originated in the Orphic mystery cult and was associated with a belief in the reincarnation of souls. They passed through many bodies of beasts and of men; the wheel of births seemed hopelessly to turn back upon itself. The expression, stripped of its Orphic concepts, became part of the language of the Hellenistic world. It occurs in the Rabbinical literature of the second century A.D. with the meaning "the wheel of fate" which is in God's hand. In Jas it probably means the entire course of life from birth to death. This is the common interpretation of both ancient and modern commentators of Jas. The NAB translation: "Its flames encircle our course from birth" expresses Jas' meaning much better than the RSV rendition "the cycle of nature." The evil power of the tongue, James concludes, is devilish: it is "set on fire by hell."

The comparison of the tongue with a firebrand is frequent in the Old Testament and in hellenistic literature, especially in diatribes. E.g. Prov 16:27 "A worthless man plots evil, and his speech is like a scorching fire"; Prov 26:21 "As charcoal to hot embers and wood to fire, so is a quarrelsome man for kindling strife." James' treatment of the evils of the tongue was probably suggested by Sir 28:12-26.

James laments in verses 7 and 8 the difficulty of curbing the tongue. Mankind, in the course of its history, has succeeded in taming beasts, birds, reptiles and sea creatures but "no human can tame the tongue – a restless evil, full of deadly poison." The comparison of the tongue to a venomous serpent is an Old Testament metaphor, e.g. Ps 140:3: "They make their tongue sharp as a serpent's, and under their lips is the poison of vipers."

The Pelagians attempted to weaken the pessimistic conclusion of James "no human being can tame the tongue" by turning the statement into a question: "Can any human being tame the tongue"? To this St. Augustine responded: "he does not say no one can tame the tongue, but no human being. We declare that by the mercy of God, with the help of God, by the grace of God it can be mastered." (*De natura et gratia XV*).

Verses 9-12 offer strong support to those who maintain that the author of Jas was a Jewish-Christian. They express concepts that are thoroughly Jewish and which occur frequently in Jewish literature, both in Old Testament and in non-canonical writings such as the Testament of Benjamin and the rule of the Qumran Community to which we owe the Dead Sea Scrolls. E.g. Ps 62:4 "They bless with their mouths, but inwardly they curse"; Sir 5:13 "Glory and dishonor come from speaking, and a man's tongue is his downfall." 1QS, X, 21-24: "I shall not keep Belial in my heart; no man shall hear, coming forth from my mouth futile words, and guilty deceits, falsehoods and lies shall not be found upon my lips. The fruit of holiness shall be upon my tongue and abominations shall not be found thereon. I shall open my mouth with thankful praise, my tongue shall tell forever the mercies of God and the treachery of men until they turn back from their sins. I shall shut out vain things from my lips, impurities and falsehoods from the knowledge of my heart." (Translation of Géza Vermes, *Discovery In The Judean Desert*, p. 154).

Jesus writes in the first person plural "we bless; we curse," because he describes an experience which every honest person knows to be his own. When we participate in the Church's worship and in our own private prayer, we employ our tongues to praise God our Father; but, when angry and hurt, we use the same tongues to curse men and women who have been created in God's own image (Gen 1:27). This shocking paradox of human speech is a favorite motif of Jewish moral exhortation. It is met frequently in the rabbinical literature; e.g. a rabbinical commentary on Ex 20:26; "thou shalt not express contempt for thy neighbor who was created in the image of God"; and a comment on Gen: "if you despise your neighbor, know whom you are despising: he has been created in the image of God." And in the popular book of Enoch, which some Christians (e.g. Jude 14) revered as Scripture, we read: "Blessed is he who opens his mouth to praise the Lord; cursed is he who opens his mouth to abuse his neighbor! Cursed is he who makes contemptible a creature of the Lord! With his own hand the Lord created mankind and made its countenance like to His . . . Whoever despises the face of a man, despises the face of the Lord." (Hen. slav. 52:1,2,6; 44:1). James clinches his argument by an appeal to nature expressed in questions that can be answered only in the negative: Fresh water and brackish water do not flow from the same spring; neither the sea nor a salt water river can yield fresh water; a fig tree can not bear olives, nor can a grapevine produce figs. This last example reminds us of Jesus' saying in the Sermon on the Mount, Mt 7:16.

THE MARKS OF TRUE WISDOM.
3:13-18.

> [13]Who is wise and understanding among you? By his good life let him show his works in the meekness of

wisdom. [14]But if you have bitter jealousy and selfish ambition in your hearts, do not boast and be false to the truth. [15]This wisdom is not such as comes down from above, but is earthly, unspiritual, devilish. [16]For where jealousy and selfish ambition exist, there will be disorder and every vile practice. [17]But the wisdom from above is first pure, then peaceable, gentle, open to reason, full of mercy and good fruits, without uncertainty or insincerity. [18]And the harvest of righteousness is sown in peace by those who make peace.

At first sight there seems to be no connection between this section of the epistle and the preceding section which dealt with the evils of the tongue and specifically with the sins to which teachers are prone. But, since Judaism practically identified the teacher of the congregation, the Rabbi, with the wise man, this section which describes the qualities that distinguish the truly wise from those who pretend to possess wisdom is quite in order after 3:1-12. Verse 16 which attributes disorder and vile practice to selfish ambition recalls the warning against a self-centered ambitious desire for the charism and office of teaching (3:1). James has in mind in 3:13-18 the know-it-all, self-righteous teachers who are disrupting the peace of Christian communities by their distortion of the Pauline teaching on Christian liberty. The teacher who possesses the wisdom from above, which is a gift of the Spirit, promotes peace and harmony. The genuine charismatic teacher will be recognized by the conformity of his life to the teaching of Christ which he has been called to expound. The truly wise practice what they teach. Their lives exemplify the gospel. Meekness is a distinctive characteristic of true wisdom because it is the mark of a true disciple who has learned from Jesus to be meek and humble of heart. James may be alluding to the Jesus' Sayings in Mt 11:29 and 23:2-11. Bitter jealousy, selfish ambition and arrogant boasting are the characteristic qualities of earthly, unspiritual, devilish wisdom. The earthly wise do not have "the mind

of Christ" because their standard of judgment is not the
gospel but their own selfish egoism (1 Cor 2:14-16). James
employs the same adjectives as does Paul in describing this
earthly wisdom; it is *psychikos* i.e. "natural" or "unspiritual." It esteems the gifts of the Spirit of God as folly and
cannot understand them (1 Cor 2:14). James calls this a
devilish wisdom because it flows from arrogant pride and is
the source of lies, and dissensions which destroy peace.
We are reminded of the disorders and immoralities of the
Corinthian church which Paul seems to regard as the
evil fruit of the factions which had destroyed the unity and
peace of the community (cf. 1 Cor 11:17-22; 1:11-12; 3:1-4).
Although St. Clement of Rome probably did not know the
Epistle of James, his authentic letter to the Corinthians
(1 Clement) written about 96 A.D., on the occasion of a
schism which had destroyed the unity of that church, contains a passage that may serve as an excellent commentary
on this section of James: "And so brothers, it is right and
holy for us to be obedient to God rather than to follow
those who in arrogance and insubordination are the
leaders in abominable jealousy. For we shall suffer no
ordinary harm, but run a very great risk, if we rashly
entrust ourselves to the designs of men who aim at strife
and sedition, to alienate us from what is right. Let us be
kind to one another after the model of the compassion and
sweetness of Him who made us" (1 Clem 14:1-3).

James then proceeds to enumerate the qualities of the
wisdom from above, the gift of the Spirit. It is first of all
"pure." The Greek word used by Jas., *agne*, occurs in the
Greek version of the Old Testament as a translation of
several Hebrew words. It means pure, innocent, straight-
forward, right. The meaning James attaches to *agne* in
verse 17 is probably that given to the word in Prov 21:8:
"the way of the guilty is crooked, but the conduct of the
pure is right," or as James read it in his Greek Old Testament,
"To the crooked God sends crooked ways; for His works are
pure and straight." Ps 12:7 (LXX, 11:7) declares that the

words of the Lord are *agnia*, like "silver refined in a cru-
cible," i.e. genuine, true, undefiled by any deceit or ambiguity. The wisdom from above does not deceive in any
way whatsoever; it is free of all hypocrisy and self-seeking.
It promotes peace; it is "gentle" (*epieikes*), i.e. in applying
law it moderates rigorous justice by sympathetic understanding of excusing of mitigating circumstances. "Lenient"
may be a more accurate translation of *epieikes* than "gentle."
The heavenly wisdom is also "open to reason" i.e. it listens
with an open mind and is docile. It is full of mercy and good
deeds; it is free of prejudice and favoritism (a better translation of the Greek word *adiakritos* in this context than
"without certainty"); it is sincere.

James concludes this chapter which has dealt with sins
of speech and earthly, devilish wisdom with a proverb
that extols "the harvest of righteousness" which is the
fruit of the peacemakers who possess the wisdom from
above. We are reminded of similar descriptions of the "fruit
of wisdom" and the "fruit of the Spirit" in the Book of
Sirach and in Paul's letter to the Galatians. Sir 1:16 "To fear
the Lord is wisdom's full measure; she satisfies men with her
fruits." Gal 5:22 "But the fruit of the Spirit is love, joy,
peace, patience, kindness, goodness, faithfulness, gentle-
ness, self-control."

PEACE OR DISCORD:
GOD OR THE WORLD.
4:1-12.

4 What causes wars, and what causes fightings among
you? Is it not your passions that are at war in your members? [2]You desire and do not have; so you kill. And you
covet and cannot obtain; so you fight and wage war. You
do not have, because you do not ask. [3]You ask and do not
receive, because you ask wrongly, to spend it on your
passions. [4]Unfaithful creatures! Do you not know that
friendship with the world is enmity with God? Therefore

whoever wishes to be a friend of the world makes himself an enemy of God. [5]Or do you suppose it is in vain that the scripture says, "He yearns jealously over the spirit which he has made to dwell in us"? [6]But he gives more grace; therefore it says, "God opposes the proud, but gives grace to the humble." [7]Submit yourselves therefore to God. Resist the devil and he will flee from you. [8]Draw near to God and he will draw near to you. Cleanse your hands, you sinners, and purify your hearts, you men of double mind. [9]Be wretched and mourn and weep. Let your laughter be turned to mourning and your joy to dejection. [10]Humble yourselves before the Lord and he will exalt you.

[11]Do not speak evil against one another, brethren. He that speaks evil against a brother or judges his brother, speaks evil against the law and judges the law. But if you judge the law, you are not a doer of the law but a judge. [12]There is one lawgiver and judge, he who is able to save and to destroy. But who are you that you judge your neighbor?

In the preceding chapter James described the destructive activities of the tongue. He seems to have had in mind the evils caused by the self-appointed, self-righteous teachers who boasted that they were wise men. Their wisdom, James declared, was earthly and devilish. He concluded with a reference to the harvest of righteousness, the peace and harmony produced by those who possess the wisdom from above which is God's gift to the humble. In this first section of chapter 4 he addresses himself to the question: why are there factions, disputes and conflicts in the Christian communities? Themes treated earlier in the letter are touched on again, e.g. prayer (4:2 cmp 1:6), love of the world (4:4 cmp 1:27), humility (4:6,9 cmp 1:9), love of the neighbor (4:11 cmp 2:13,15). The section is framed by the opening question, "what causes wars, and what causes fightings among you"? and by the concluding exhortation, "do not speak evil against one another brethren . . . who are you that you judge your neighbor"? This framework gives a certain unity to what otherwise might seem to be a haphazard collection of moral maxims.

4:1-3. The key word of these verses is "passions" which occurs in verses 1 and 3, giving the passage a unity through the rhetorical device called "inclusion." The phrase "among you" clearly indicates that "the wars and fightings" which James has in mind are the quarrels, the wranglings, the angry disputes which are destroying the peace of some of the christian communities and splitting them into warring factions. The strong language employed by James would seem to imply that on occasion the rancor harbored by the opposing factions led to angry quarrels and even to fighting. Clement of Rome uses the word war (*polemos*) and other words signifying violent political upheavals to describe the evils occasioned by the schism in the church of Corinth, e.g. "strife and sedition, persecution and anarchy, war and captivity" 1 Clem 3:2. The immediate cause of the "wars and fightings" among the communities addressed by James is the pernicious activity of the false teachers. But he is inquiring into the root cause of these evils. He answers, using a rhetorical question, that in the final analysis the cause of the destruction of the unity and peace of the communities is "the passions that are at war in your members." Although he does not specify explicitly "the passions" at war within Christians he leaves no doubt (verses 2-4) that like 2 Pt 1:11 he is referring to "the passions of the flesh that wage war against your soul." The appetites and desires that flow from self-centered egoism war against the Christian conscience, right judgment, and love that should always motivate the disciples of Christ. Surrender to these selfish desires leads to envy of the material possessions of others and occasions quarreling and strife. 1 Clem 3:4 expresses the same thought as James. "For this reason," Clement tells the Corinthians, "piety and peace are far removed, because everyone has abandoned the fear of God and lost the clear vision which faith affords, and nobody regulates his conduct by the norms of His commandments, or tries to make his life worthy of Christ. On the contrary, everyone follows the appetites of his depraved heart, for they have absorbed that unjust and unholy jealousy through which 'death came into the world.'" (The reference is to Wis 2:24.)

Verses 2 and 3 describe "the wars and fightings of the passions." A literal translation of the Greek text reads as follows: "You desire and do not have; you kill and covet and you cannot obtain; you fight and wage war. You do not have because you do not ask; you ask and do not receive, because you ask wrongly, to spend it on your passions." The RSV and other modern translations (e.g. NAB) join "you kill" with the first phrase and by introducing the conjunction "so" interpret the killing as a result of unsatisfied desire. The phrase "you fight and wage war" is interpreted in the same way. Some exegetes, Catholic and Protestant, following the great Renaissance scholar Erasmus, replace "you kill" (*phonuete*) by "you are jealous" (*pthonuete*); "you are jealous and you covet." These exegetes point out that "you covet" is insipid and weak following "you kill." And they cannot bring themselves to believe that the quarrels in the christian communities have resulted in murder. The decisive argument against these exegetes is the fact that all the manuscripts of the Epistles of James read *phonuete*, "you kill." This unanimity of the Greek manuscripts and ancient versions establishes the certainty of the reading "you kill." The expression is difficult, indeed startling, and if taken literally it is horrible. But this does not warrant changing the text. Does James actually accuse the factious Christians of murder? The wisdom literature of Judaism lists murder among the evil effects of sins of speech, and in the tradition of Judaism jealousy and murder are frequently linked together. The book of Sirach, a favorite source of James, 28:17-18 declares: "The blow of a whip raises a welt, but a blow of the tongue crushes the bones. Many have fallen by the edge of the sword, but not so many as have fallen because of the tongue." James, like Sirach, probably attaches a figurative meaning to the expression "you kill." Angry jealousy erupts in vicious slander and detraction which destroys the reputation, the happiness, i.e. the lives of its victims.

James' readers do not possess the good things they yearn for because they do not pray properly. Jesus declared: "everyone who asks receives" (Mt 7:28). James' readers do not receive because they ask wrongly, to spend it on their passions. They pray only for the things which will satisfy those desires which are the fruit of "the friendship of the world." The translation "unfaithful creatures!" (v.4) fails to express the specific nuance of the Greek word employed by James, *moichalides*, "adulteresses." Ever since the eighth century B.C. prophet Hosea used the marriage union of husband and wife as an analogue of the covenant union of God with Israel apostasy from God was stigmatized as adultery. Unfaithful Israel, Yahweh's spouse, went awhoring after strange gods (cf. Is 1:21; Jer 2:20; 3:6-10, Ezek 16:23-34). Jesus employed the prophetic language when he called his unbelieving contemporaries "an evil and adulterous generation" (Mt 12:39; 16:4; Mk 8:38). Paul speaks of the church as the bride of Christ. He writes to the Corinthians: "I feel a divine jealousy for you, for I betrothed you to Christ to present you as a pure bride to her one husband. But I am afraid that as the serpent deceived Eve by his cunning, your thoughts will be led astray from a sincere and pure devotion to Christ" (2 Cor 11:2-3; cf. also Eph 5:22-24; Rev 19:7; 21:9). In Jas "friendship with the world," i.e. love of the world, has the same pejorative ethical meaning that is given to the expression in the Johannine writings; cf. e.g. 1 Jn 2:15-16 "Do not love the world or the things in the world. If anyone loves the world, love for the Father is not in him. For all that is in the world, the lust of the flesh and the lust of the eyes and the pride of life, is not of the Father but is of the world." James insisted in 1:27 that true religion imposes the obligation "to keep oneself unstained from the world." The material universe is good. "And God saw everything that he had made, and behold it was very good" (Gen 1:31). God's good creation becomes an occasion of evil when self-centered man abuses it to satisfy his selfish desires, his disordered appetites. Then, in the language of Paul, creation is "subjected to futility" and sinful man becomes an enemy of God (Rom 8:20). James echoes in v.4 the saying of Jesus in the Sermon on the Mount: "No one can serve two masters; for either he will hate the one and love the other, or he will be devoted to the one and despise the other. You cannot serve God and mammon" (Mt 6:24).

Because of the ambiguity of the language verse 5 is very difficult and has taxed the ingenuity of interpreters. The opening phrase "Or do you suppose it is in vain that the scripture says" indicates very clearly that the following citation is adduced in support of the statement that friendship of the world is incompatible with love of God and that he who "wishes to be a friend of the world makes himself an enemy of God." In the Greek text the spirit (*to pneuma*) can be either the subject or the object of the verb "yearns." The scriptural citation of verse 6 "God resists the proud etc." indicates beyond all doubt that God is also the subject expressed by the pronoun of the preceding sentence, "But he gives more grace" (literally "a greater gift"). Consequently since the grace, or greater gift, of verse 6 is contrasted with the gift of which verse 5 speaks, the subject of verse 5 must also be God, and "the spirit" which is God's gift to man is the object of God's jealous desire. The translation of RSV "He (i.e. God) yearns jealously over the spirit which he has made to dwell in us" is an excellent translation of the Greek text. What spirit given by God to man is the object of the divine jealousy? The holy Spirit? or the "breath of life," in our language "the soul"? Verse 6 declares that the humble receive from God a greater gift than "the spirit" mentioned in the preceding verse. Consequently, the spirit of verse 5 cannot mean the holy Spirit which is the greatest gift God gives. Therefore most interpreters rightly understand the spirit, which is the object of God's jealous desire, to refer to "the breath of life," "the soul" (cf. Gn 2:7). No biblical writing contains the text which James adduces as a scriptural citation. Perhaps he is expressing in the form of a proverb (the rhythm of the Greek text is reminiscent of a hexameter, as is also 1:17) a theme which is met frequently in the Old Testament. A number of Old Testament passages speak of God's jealous love for his people; e.g. Ex 34:14 "for you shall worship no other god, for the Lord whose name is Jealous, is a jealous God" (cf. also Ex 20:5; Dt 4:24; 5:9; 6:15; Jos 24:19; Ezek 5:13; 16:38). Implied in all these passages is the marriage symbol of the Covenant. God's jealousy is like that of a husband's love for his wife. He will not share her with another. The jealousy of God for his people expresses negatively the commandment given to Israel which Jesus called the great and first commandment: "You shall love the Lord your God with all your heart, and with all your soul, and with all your mind" (Mt 22:37-38; Dt 6:5).

It is also quite probable that the source of James' citation may be an apocryphal writing which he regarded as sacred scripture. The author of the Epistle of Jude appeals to two apocryphal writings just as he would to biblical books; verse 9 is an allusion to the Assumption of Moses, and verses 14 and 15 are a citation from The Book of Enoch. Another apocryphal writing, the Book of Jubilees known also as the Apocalypse of Moses, speaks of God's yearning desire for "the vessel" He has created. It tells how the dying Adam asks his wife Eve to pray to God "until I give back my spirit into the hand of Him who gave it" (ch. 31). And in ch. 42 the dying Eve prays: "'God of all take my spirit', and immediately she surrendered her spirit to God." Spirit in these passages is the gift of life which God breathed into man at his creation (Gn 2:26). James declares that God loves man whom he has created with a jealous love that will tolerate no rival. He who loves the world violates the love and disregards the just claims of the Creator.

Love of the world is really self-centered egoism, i.e.
pride (Jn 9:16). God gives a greater gift than life to the
humble, i.e. to those who recognize their absolute dependence on him and love him with all their heart, mind and
strength. James cites the Greek version of Prov 3:34 which
declares that only the humble who acknowledge their
nothingness and their dependence on God are the recipients
of his grace. What is the gift greater than life which God
gives to the humble? In the context of the epistle it is the
gift of faith and the promise of inheriting the Kingdom of
God (2:5), and specifically, in the immediate context of
this section, the eschatological exaltation (4:10), i.e. the
glory of the resurrection. The First Epistle of Peter makes a
similar exhortation to humility, citing the same text of
Proverbs (3:34) and promising the same exaltation (1 Pt
5:5b-6; cf. also Mt 23:12). In verses 7-12 James exhorts his
readers to submit themselves in humble obedience to God.
"Resist the devil and he will flee from you." The seductive
attractions of the world are the temptations of the devil,
"the ruler of this world"(Jn 14:30), to draw men and women
away from their allegiance to God. In the measure in which
we draw near to God through humble prayer and obedience, he will draw near to us.

The priests of the ancient covenant were obliged to wash
their hands and their feet before entering the sanctuary to
perform their ministry. Death was the penalty for violation
of this commandment (Ex 30:19-21). The Rabbis obliged all
Jews to perform a ritual washing before eating. Jesus
changed this into an ethical command. True cleanliness
is in the heart, in a will that is obedient to God. Nothing
exterior defiles a man morally. What proceeds from the
heart, e.g. evil thoughts, fornication, theft, murder,
adultery, pride, "these are what defile a man; but to eat
with unwashed hands does not defile a man" (Mt 15:20).
The address "you sinners" clearly indicates that, like Jesus,
James gives an ethical interpretation to the precept "cleanse
your hands." He adds to this negative command the positive
exhortation, "Purify your hearts, you men of double mind."

The Greek verb *agnizein* (to purify, to cleanse) has a cultic signification in both the Old and New Testaments. It means to ritually dispose oneself for divine worship. In Ex 19:10, Jn 11:55, Acts 21:24,26 and 24:18 it refers to the purification rites that were prescribed as a preparation for participation in divine worship. In Jas as also in 1 Pt 1:22, 1 Jn 3:3, and indeed in some Old Testament texts, e.g. Ps 24:4 and Sir 38:10, the verb has an ethical signification. It refers to the interior moral dispositions required of the worshiper. James' exhortation echoes that of his favorite Old Testament book, Sirach: "Give up your faults and direct your hands aright, and cleanse your heart from all sin" (Sir 38:10). The address "you men of double mind" harks back to 1:8. A man of double mind is a person who wavers between God and the world, who compromises and tries to serve both God and mammon. Again James echoes Sirach: "Woe to timid hearts and to slack hands, and to the sinner who walks along two ways"! (Sir 2:12).

Verse 9 is a ringing call to repentance. Wanton laughter and riotous joy characterize those who love the world. Such behavior declares Sirach, is a mark of the fool (Sir 21:28) and an expression of wanton guilt (Sir 27:13). The laughter of the lovers of this world will be turned into weeping at the eschatological judgment. "Woe to you that laugh now, for you shall mourn and weep" (Lk 6:25). Repentance requires that one recognize one's wretchedness, weep for one's sinfulness and cast oneself with childlike confidence into the arms of God. These are the humble, the *anawim*, to whom Jesus has promised the Kingdom. "Blessed are those who mourn, for they shall be comforted" (Mt 6:4). So James concludes this exhortation with the Lord's promise of the joy of the Kingdom to the humble. "Blessed are the poor in spirit for theirs is the Kingdom of heaven" (Mt 6:3). "Humble yourself before the Lord and he will exalt you" (v.10).

Verses 11-12 Once again James returns to the evils occasioned by "the wars and fightings" resulting from the activities of the false teachers. The factions into which the communities are split have led Christians to slander and to sit in judgment on their brothers and sisters in Christ. Slander, defamation and backbiting are sharply condemned by both the Old and the New Testament (cf. Ps 50:20; Wis 1:10-11; Rom 1:30; 2 Cor 12:20, and especially 1 Pt which has a number of parallels to Jas, 1 Pt 2:1-12; 3:16). James points out that slander implies a judgment of one's neighbor. The slanderer sits in self-righteous judgment and condemns his victims. Thus he violates the law of love of the neighbor which, together with the law of love of God, sums up the entire law. The slanderer presumes to judge the very "royal law" itself (cf. 2:8-9). Perhaps James is recalling Prov 17:5 "He who mocks the poor insults his maker." But he goes beyond the Old Testament in his condemnation of slander. The slanderer, because of the judgment he has passed on his neighbor, usurps God's jurisdiction. He arrogantly presumes to put himself in the place of God who is both Lawgiver and Judge. The slanderer forgets completely his creatureliness, what he really is, a miserable, sinful human being who must stand before the judgment seat of God his creator. Verses 11 and 12 are a stinging condemnation of the self-righteous and arrogant presumption of those who are causing discord and wrangling in the Christian communities.

THE FOLLY OF THOSE WHO PLAN THEIR LIVES WITHOUT DEPENDANCE ON GOD. 4:13-17.

[13]Come now, you who say, "Today or tomorrow we will go into such and such a town and spend a year there and trade and get gain"; [14]whereas you do not know about tomorrow. What is your life? For you are a mist that appears for a little time and then vanishes. [15]Instead you ought to say, "If the Lord wills, we shall live and we shall do this or that." [16]As it is, you boast in your arrogance. All such boasting is evil. [17]Whoever knows what is right to do and fails to do it, for him it is sin.

In this warning to merchants who, intent on profit, plan their travels a year in advance without any consideration of their dependance on God, James takes up a traditional theme of the Old Testament hortatory literature; e.g. Sir 11:18-19 "There is a man who is rich through his diligence and self-denial, and this is the reward allotted to him: when he says, 'I have found rest, and now I shall enjoy my goods!' he does not know how much time will pass until he leaves them to others and dies." Perhaps James is also thinking of Jesus' parable about the foolish farmer who, when he had an abundant harvest, decided to build larger barns to store his grain and goods and planned to enjoy his wealth. "And I will say to my soul, 'Soul, you have ample goods laid up for many years; take your ease, eat, drink, be merry.' But God said to him, 'Fool! This night your soul is required of you; and the things you have prepared, whose will they be?' So is he who lays up treasure for himself, and is not rich toward God" (Lk 12:19-21).

We are mortal. Our continuance in existence depends on God the giver and Lord of life. In all our planning there must be at least the implied condition "If God so wills." Thus Paul writes to the Corinthians, "I will come to you soon, if the Lord wills" (1 Cor 4:19); and "I hope to spend some time with you, if the Lord permits" (1 Cor 16:7; cf. also Heb 6:3 and Acts 18:21).

The Greek word *alazoneia*, translated "arrogance" in verse 16, and which James associates with boasting, is enumerated in 1 Jn 2:16 (where it is translated "pride of life") among the three evils of the world in its ethical signification as rival to the love of God. 1 Jn 2:15-17: "Do not love the world or the things in the world. If anyone loves the world, love for the Father is not in him. For all that is in the world, the lust of the flesh and the lust of the eyes and the pride of life, is not of the Father but is of the world. And the world passes away, and the lust of it; but he who does the will of God abides forever." For James "the pride of life" is the arrogant boasting of those who love the world

and seek their happiness without recognizing their dependance on God. James' warning to the self-seeking merchants
is connected rather loosely to his warning against love of
the world in verses 4-8. This entire section concludes with a
proverb expressing a general moral truth: to deliberately
fail to do what one knows is right is sinful (Lk 12:47;
2 Pt 2:21).

A WARNING TO THE RICH.
5:1-6.

> **5** Come now, you rich, weep and howl for the miseries
> that are coming upon you. ²Your riches have rotted and
> your garments are moth-eaten. ³Your gold and silver
> have rusted, and their rust will be evidence against you
> and will eat your flesh like fire. You have laid up treasure
> for the last days. ⁴Behold, the wages of the laborers who
> mowed your fields, which you kept back by fraud, cry
> out; and the cries of the harvesters have reached the
> ears of the Lord of hosts. ⁵You have lived on the earth
> in luxury and in pleasure; you have fattened your hearts
> in a day of slaughter. ⁶You have condemned, you have
> killed the righteous man; he does not resist you.

James inveighs with sharp invective against the rich
landowners who exploit the poor. He begins with the same
imperative with which he addressed the merchants who
arrogantly plan their lives without recognizing their dependance on God: "Come now." The language and content of this terrible threat to the unjust rich is borrowed
from the Old Testament prophets and from the Sayings
of Jesus. The opening command "weep and howl" echoes
the imperatives with which the prophets (in the Greek
version of the Old Testament) begin their oracles of doom.
In his prediction of the destruction of Babylon (Is 13:6)
the prophet commands the Babylonians "howl, for the day
of the Lord is near"; and the Greek version of Is 15:3 (the
oracle against Moab) is very similar to Jas 5:1, "howl, all

of you with weeping" (cf. also Jer 31:20; Ezek 21:17; Zech 11:2). The "woes," which in Luke's Sermon on the Plain follow the beatitudes, are in the same prophetic tradition. "But woe to you that are rich, for you have received your consolation" (Lk 6:24). And James' language in verse 2 and 3 reminds us of Jesus' Saying in the Sermon on the Mount: "Do not lay up for yourselves treasures on earth, where moth and rust consume and where thieves break in and steal" (Mt 6:19). There is no doubt that the coming eschatological Day of Judgment has motivated James' dire threats. This is clearly stated in the ironic language of verses 3 and 6. The unjust, self-indulgent rich have laid up "treasure" for the last days. By their luxurious living they have fattened themselves for a day of slaughter. The prophets describe God's judgment and punishment of the wicked as a slaughter, e.g. Isaiah's oracle against Edom: "For my sword has drunk its fill in the heavens; behold, it descends for judgment upon Edom, the people I have doomed. The Lord has a sword; it is sated with blood, it is gorged with fat . . . For the Lord has a sacrifice in Bozrah, a great slaughter in the land of Edom" (Is 34:5-6; cf. also Jer 12:3; 46:10). The New Testament book of Apocalypse describes with frightening metaphors the slaughter of the great day of the eschatological judgment (cf. Apoc 19:17-21).

The perfect tense of the verbs in verses 2 and 3 presents a problem. "Your riches have rotted and your garments are moth-eaten. Your gold and silver have rusted." James seems to imply that the miseries predicted in verse 1 have already fallen upon the rich. A number of exegetes interpret these verbs as "prophetic perfects" which really refer to future events but are expressed with the perfect tense because the prophet in his "vision" sees them as already realized. This use of the perfect tense is quite frequent in the Old Testament prophetic writings. If James were employing the prophetic perfect he would be saying that at the day of judgment all the stored up treasures and wealth of the rich will be worthless. But there is difficulty with this interpretation. James declares that when the day of judgment

comes the rust of the silver and gold of the rich will testify
against them and will consume their flesh like fire. So the
rust already exists before the coming of judgment day. The
entire context of the passage, especially the ironic concluding sentence of verse 3, "You have laid up treasure for
the last days," supports the interpretation that the rich will
be condemned because, instead of helping the poor from
their wealth, they selfishly stored it away for themselves.
The treasure they have laid up for the last days is rust that
will witness against them on judgment day. They laid up
"treasures on earth where moth and rust consume" (Mt
6:19). They did not heed Jesus' counsel: "And I tell you,
make friends for yourselves by means of unrighteous
mammon, so that when it fails they may receive you into
the eternal habitations" (Lk 16:9). Of course silver and
gold do not rust but, lying stored away in coffers they are
as useless as rusted iron. On the day of judgment this "rust"
which they had stored away to guarantee their comfortable
living will consume them like fire. James here employs a
biblical metaphor for the punishment of the wicked; e.g.
Judith 16:17 "Woe to the nations that rise up against my
people! The Lord God Almighty will take vengeance on
them in the day of judgment; fire and worms he will give to
their flesh; they shall weep in pain forever" (cf. also Ps
21:5-7; Is 66:24 and Jesus' Sayings in Mt 5:22; 7:19; 13:50).

The rich landowners are guilty of a crime which like the
blood of the murdered Abel cries to heaven for vengeance.
The cries of the laborers who have been defrauded of their
just wages are heard by God the Almighty Lord of the
heavenly armies. He will inflict just punishment on their
rich oppressors. James probably has in mind the text of
Sirach: "The bread of the needy is the life of the poor;
whoever deprives them of it is a man of blood. To take away
a neighbor's living is to murder him; to deprive an employee
of his wages is to shed blood" (Sir 34:21-22; cf. also Dt
24:14-15; Lev 19:13). Like the rich man in Jesus' parable
(Lk 16:19-31) who clothed himself in purple and fine linen
and feasted sumptuously every day while poor Lazarus

lay at his gate with dogs licking his sores, the unjust wealthy landowners by their luxurious dissipated lives have fattened their "hearts," like unsuspecting sheep, for the day of slaughter, the Day of the Lord when their laughter will be turned into mourning and their injustices severely punished. The heart is, in the Old Testament, a metaphor for the will. The willful self-indulgence of the rich has made them the objects of God's wrath. James concludes this invective against the wealthy exploiters of the poor with an allusion to the Book of Wisdom: "You have condemned, you have killed the righteous man; he does not resist you" (cf. Wis 2:18-20). "The righteous man" (*ho dikaios*) is a collective singular signifying all the righteous poor victims of the wicked wealthy. The Greek version of Ps 37 (in the LXX Ps 36) verses 12-13 and 17 offers an excellent example of this collective use of "the righteous man," "The wicked man plots against the righteous man (sing. *ton dikaion*) and gnashes his teeth against him" (12-13); "For the arms (i.e. the power) of sinners (plural) will be broken, but the Lord supports the righteous (plural, *tous dikaious*)" (17). In a number of New Testament texts "the righteous" or "the just one" (*ho dikaios*) is a title of Jesus the Messiah, e.g. Acts 3:14; 7:52; 22:14; 1 Pt 3:18; 1 Jn 2:1,29; 3:7). It is probable that in employing the singular number and speaking of the righteous man who does not resist his persecutor. James may have been thinking of Jesus in his Passion, the exemplar of all who suffer at the hands of the wicked. However, the present tense "he does not resist you" clearly indicates that he is not referring only to Jesus. This entire section of the epistle expresses a traditional theme of the Anawim theology of the Old Testament and of Jesus' teaching (cf. Amos 5:12; Ps 10:8-10; Wis 2:6-22; Lk 6:24-25; 1 Pt 4:12-14; Mt 5:3-11).

PATIENCE: THE LORD IS COMING.
5:7-11.

> [7]Be patient, therefore, brethren, until the coming of the Lord. Behold, the farmer waits for the precious fruit

of the earth, being patient over it until it receives the
early and the late rain. ⁸You also be patient. Establish
your hearts, for the coming of the Lord is at hand. ⁹Do
not grumble, brethren, against one another, that you may
not be judged; behold, the Judge is standing at the doors.
¹⁰As an example of suffering and patience, brethren,
take the prophets who spoke in the name of the Lord.
¹¹Behold, we call those happy who were steadfast. You
have heard of the steadfastness of Job, and you have
seen the purpose of the Lord, how the Lord is compas-
sionate and merciful.

The theme of the coming of the Risen Lord to inaugurate
the glorious Kingdom of God and to judge all mankind
links this section of the epistle with the preceding invective
against the unjust rich. James employs the word *parousia*
(advent, coming) which, because of its association with an
official visit of the Roman emperor to a city or a province,
was adopted by Greek-speaking Christians as the proper
term for the return of Christ, the King and Lord of glory,
at the end of time to usher in the glorious Kingdom of God
and to judge all mankind (cf. 1 Thess 4:15; Mt 24:3; in both
these texts the word "coming" is, as in James, a translation
of the Greek word *parousia*). The Epistle of James says
nothing about the time of the Lord's coming and there is not
the slightest hint that the Christians to whom it was written
were deeply disturbed because of the delay of the Parousia
as, e.g. were the addressees of Second Peter (2 Pt 3:3-10). It
is a basic Christian belief expressed in many passages of
the New Testament that "the last days" and "the age to
come" began with the Lord's Resurrection and gift of the
Spirit. Speculation on the time of the Parousia is not only
futile, but is forbidden. No one knows the day and the hour
which has been fixed by the Father (Mk 13:32-33; Acts 1:7).
The Day of the Lord will come unexpectedly, like "a thief
in the night." James' expressions "the coming of the Lord

is at hand" and "the judge is standing at the doors" stress the sureness of Christian faith and hope in the Lord's return and are an implicit exhortation to be ever ready to meet him for he may come at any moment (cf. Mt 24:42-44). Just as the farmer waits patiently for "the precious fruit of the earth," knowing that the seed he has sown will not sprout and fructify until the soil has received the early (winter) and the later (spring) rains, so the christian must patiently endure trials and persecutions, knowing that through the testing of his faith and steadfast perseverance the new life to which he was begotten when he believed in the gospel will be brought to full maturity, to the eternal life of the glorious Kingdom (cf. Jas 1:2-4; 18:2-5).

In verse 9 James interjects a warning against passing judgment on others. This brief interruption of the flow of his thought was occasioned by his preoccupation with the last judgment. He recalls Jesus' warning in the Sermon on the Mount: "Judge not, that you be not judged. For with what judgment you pronounce you will be judged, and the measure you give will be the measure you get" (Mt 7:1-2). Returning to his exhortation to patience, he holds up before his readers the example of the prophets of the Old Testament and of the patient Job. Perhaps he is thinking of the last beatitude of the Sermon on the Mount: "Blessed are you when men revile you and persecute you and utter all kinds of evil against you falsely on my account. Rejoice and be glad, for your reward is great in heaven, for so men persecuted the prophets who were before you"(Mt 5:11-12). The sentence "you have seen the purpose of the Lord"refers to the happy ending of the story of Job. God rewarded Job's patient "steadfastness" by giving him twice as many sheep, oxen and she-asses as he had lost and blessing him with a new family of seven sons and three daughters, who were the most beautiful women in the land. Moreover he lived to enjoy his wealth and happiness to the ripe old age of one hundred and forty-four and he saw even his great grandchildren (Job 42:12-17). Most exegetes interpret the

Greek phrase of verse 11, *to telos kyriou* (lit. the end of
(the) Lord) as a reference to God's purpose in permitting
Job's afflictions. The opening sentence of the verse "behold,
we call those happy who were steadfast" and especially the
past (aorist) tense "you have seen" strongly support this
interpretation: You have seen, i.e. in the Scripture, in the
Book of Job, the end (i.e. the purpose) which God had in
allowing Satan to try Job so terribly. "Thus the Lord
blessed the latter days of Job" (because of his patient
steadfastness) "more than his earlier ones" (Job 42:12).

Some, e.g. St. Augustine, interpret the phrase "the end of
(the) Lord" as a reference to the Lord Jesus' triumph over
death in his resurrection and glorious exaltation. A few
think the phrase refers to the glorious Parousia of the Lord
Jesus. But the absence of the article before Lord in the Greek
text and the concluding appeal to the Old Testament
declarations of the Lord's (i.e. Yahweh's) compassion and
mercy are compelling arguments in favor of the interpretation "the purpose of God" (cf. Ps 111:4, "The Lord is
gracious and merciful," also Ps 103:8; Exodus 34:6).

CONCLUDING EXHORTATIONS AND RULES.
5:12-20.

> [12]But above all, my brethren, do not swear, either
> by heaven or by earth or with any other oath, but let your
> yes be yes and your no be no, that you may not fall
> under condemnation.
> [13]Is any one among you suffering? Let him pray. Is any
> cheerful? Let him sing praise. [14]Is any among you sick?
> Let him call for the elders of the church, and let them
> pray over him anointing him with oil in the name of the
> Lord; [15]and the prayer of faith will save the sick man,
> and the Lord will raise him up; and if he has committed
> sins, he will be forgiven. [16]Therefore confess your sins
> to one another, and pray for one another, that you may
> be healed. The prayer of a righteous man has great power

in its effects. [17]Elijah was a man of like nature with ourselves and he prayed fervently that it might not rain, and for three years and six months it did not rain on the earth. [18]Then he prayed again and the heaven gave rain, and the earth brought forth its fruit.

[19]My brethren, if any one among you wanders from the truth and some one brings him back, [20]let him know that whoever brings back a sinner from the error of his way will save his soul from death and will cover a multitude of sins.

These concluding verses seem, at first sight, to have no connection with the preceding admonitions. But the references to the final judgment (v.12) and to salvation (v.20), i.e. the eschatological theme so prominent in 4:12-5:11, connect this last section of the epistle, albeit loosely, to the preceding exhortations and invectives against the rich. The eschatological motif recurs again and again, like the theme of a musical composition, from beginning to end of the epistle (cf. 1:10-12; 2:5,13-14; 3:1; 4:12-14; 5:1-11). James repeatedly reminds his readers that they are mortal creatures, that their continuance in existence, their happiness and salvation depend on God to whom they must render an account of their lives. James' moral exhortations, like the ethical teaching of Jesus, are always associated with eschatology. The last judgment was a prominent feature of Jesus' preaching. He spoke of his coming unexpectedly, on a day and at an hour known only to the Father, to judge mankind. He exhorted his followers to be patient and watchful, always prepared to receive him whenever he might come. Because of the prominence and unifying function of the eschatological motif in Jas it is difficult to accept the opinion of many modern commentators who maintain that there is very little, if any, Christian theology in the epistle, that it is simply a loose collection of moral maxims traditional to the hortatory literature of Judaism with some input from the ethical literature of the

Hellenistic world, e.g. the popular Stoic writings. Certainly eschatology is prominent in Christian theology. One gets the impression that many commentators identify christian theology exclusively with Christology. Does not the christian teaching on the Lord's Parousia belong to Christology? This doctrine is intimately associated with belief in the Resurrection of Jesus, with "the faith of our Lord Jesus Christ, the Lord of glory" (2:2).

The phrase with which James introduces his admonition against useless oaths, "but above all," does not mean that his exhortation against swearing must take precedence over all the admonitions already given. It is simply an introductory expression proper to the epistolary style of Hellenism and means: "I must not forget to write also this admonition." James' admonition against swearing is similar both in content and wording to Jesus' prohibition in the Sermon on the Mount (Mt 5:34-37). Christians must be truthful and sincere in their relations with others. All double-talk, equivocation and lying will be condemned by the divine judge. This history of Christianity shows that the New Testament prohibition of swearing was not applied (except in a few sects like the Quakers) to oaths prescribed by competent civil or ecclesiastical authorities; e.g. oaths demanded of witnesses in court proceedings, and the oath of loyalty to the Constitution prescribed for public officials. Mt 5:34-37 and Jas 5:12 condemn the practice prevalent in their contemporary Judaism of needless swearing, of buttressing almost every statement in ordinary conversation with an oath. James' favorite Old Testament writing, The Book of Sirach, inveighs against this practice: "Do not accustom your mouth to oaths, and do not habitually utter the name of the Holy One; for as a servant who is continually examined under torture will not lack bruises, so also the man who always swears and utters the Name will not be cleansed from sin. A man who swears many oaths will be filled with iniquity, and the scourge will not leave his house . . . if he has sworn needlessly, he will not be justified, for his house will be filled with calamities" (Sir

23:9-11). The Essene Community of Qumran to which we owe the Dead Sea Scrolls renounced all oath-taking except that prescribed for the novice on his entry into the community. The Damascus Document, also an Essene writing, permits only oaths required in court proceedings. The Rabbinical writings also condemn the prevalent Jewish practice of swearing needlessly. When Judaism ceased to utter the divine name Yahweh, oaths were sworn by divine titles such as Adonai (Lord), Shaddai (the Almighty) or by circumlocutions like "the Name," "by heaven," or "by the Temple" etc., and the practice of swearing in matters of little or no importance became widespread. James warns against this needless swearing.

"Is anyone among you suffering? Let him pray. Is any cheerful? Let him sing praise" (v.13). Like the ebb and flow of the tide human existence is a succession of trials and joys. With Jesus who told his disciples that "they ought always to pray and not lost heart" (Lk 18:1), James exhorts the suffering (lit. one who undergoes hardship) to turn to God for help and comfort. The "cheerful" (lit. one who is happy) should thank God with joyful song. It is not clear whether James has in mind private expressions of joyful thanks such as we find in the Psalter (e.g. Ps 30:13) or hymns sung in the presence of and perhaps with the assembled community (e.g. Ps 33:2-3; Eph 5:19-20). He probably intends that both the prayer of the suffering and the thanksgiving of the cheerful be expressed both privately and in the liturgical assembly.

James now turns his attention to the sick members of the christian communities. His language makes it quite clear that he is speaking of rather serious illnesses, not the ordinary indispositions to which even the habitually strong and healthy are subject. The sick person is described as weary, exhausted, worn out, and since he is instructed to summon the elders of the church to come to him, it seems that he is too ill to leave his home. The qualifying genitive "of the church" indicates that "the elders" are men who hold an office in the community. James is not referring to charismatics who possess the gift of healing (cf. 1 Cor 12:9,28,30). The churches addressed by James had the office of the presbyterate which existed at an early date in the mother church of Jerusalem (Acts 11:30; 14:23; 15:2 etc.), and at the turn of the first century A.D. in the churches which received the Pastoral Epistles. We know from the Pastoral Epistles, and also from Acts, that the holders of this ecclesial office were called *episkopoi* (bishops, i.e. overseers or guardians) as well as *presbyteroi* (elders) (cf. 1 Tim 5:1-7,17; Titus 1:5,7; Acts 20:17,28). The Church of Philippi, which had been founded by Paul, also had this ecclesial office. Paul addressed his epistle to the Philippians "to all the saints in Christ Jesus who are at Philippi, with the bishops (*episkopoi*) and deacons" (Phil 1:1). The elders of the Pastoral Epistles were the leaders of their churches responsible for community administration and the ordination, by laying on of their hands, of elders and deacons. Teaching, preaching and presiding over the community's worship are listed among their duties. Their primary concern was to hold on firmly to "the deposit," i.e. the christian teaching and doctrine that was received from the apostles. The elders were the guardians of orthodoxy. The First Epistle of Peter describes the elders as shepherds of the flock of God (1 Pt 5:1).

Visiting the sick is a good work highly esteemed and praised in Judaism; e.g. Sir 7:35: "Do not shrink from visiting a sick man, because for such deeds you will be loved." The Talmud recommends prayer for the sick: "He who visits the sick should not merely sit on a bed or a chair, but he should wrap himself in his cloak and implore God to take pity on the sick person" (Shabbath 13). In Mt 25:36-46 visiting the sick is declared to be an act of loving kindness shown to Christ himself.

The ancients attributed a therapeutic power to oil. It was used especially for the healing of wounds, e.g. Is 1:6 and Lk 10:33-34. An anointing with oil was a prominent feature of the ancient Hebrew ritual for the cleansing of leprosy (cf. Lev 14:10-32).

The elders of the church pray over the sick person and anoint him/her with oil "in the name of the Lord." In the usage of the New Testament this phrase refers to the invocation of the name of Jesus Christ, the Lord of the Church (cf. Acts 3:6; 4:10; 9:28; 1 Cor 5:4; 6:11; Phil 2:10; Eph 5:20; Col 3:17; 2 Thess 3:6). The elders in their prayer over the sick person invoke the Lord Jesus. The efficacy of the anointing is attributed not to the oil itself but to the prayer made with faith in the goodness and power of the Lord whose name is invoked. In the New Testament the phrase "by the name of the Lord" is synonymous with "by the power of the Lord." For example, in Acts 4:7-10 the high priest and the Jewish authorities ask Peter "by what power or by what name" he had healed the lame beggar. Peter answered, "be it known to you all and to all the people of Israel, that by the name of Jesus Christ of Nazareth, whom you crucified, whom God raised from the dead, by him this man is standing before you well." So, also, James attributes the effects of the anointing of the sick, namely restoration to health and forgiveness of sins, to the power of Christ the Lord.

The prayer of faith James declares will *save* the sick person, and the Lord will *raise* him up; and if he has committed sins, he will be *forgiven*. The future tense of the three verbs raises a question: Is James giving these verbs an eschatological meaning? Is he speaking of salvation, resurrection from the dead, and forgiveness at the last judgment? Or, is he speaking of restoration to bodily and spiritual health here and now? In the New Testament the verbs "to save" (*sozein*) and "to raise up" (*egeirein*) may refer to final salvation and the resurrection from the dead, or to the healing of physical illnesses and afflictions. The context in which the verbs occur determines the meaning intended. In four passages James gives the verb "to save" an eschatological meaning; 1:21; 2:14; 4:12; 5:20. But the context of the anointing of the sick clearly indicates that "to save" and "to raise up" should be understood to refer to the restoration to health. Both verbs are used frequently in the New

Testament narratives of Jesus' healing miracles; e.g. Mt 9:21, the woman suffering from hemorrhage said to herself, 'if I only touch his garment, I shall be made well' (lit. 'I shall be saved'). And note the parallel between Jesus' response to the woman: "Take heart, daughter; your faith has made you well" (lit. has saved you) and James' statement that "the prayer of faith will save the sick man" (cf. also Mk 5:28,34; 6:56; 10:52; Lk 8:48, in all these passages the healing of the afflicted is expressed by the verb "to save"). "To raise up" is employed with the same meaning, e.g. Mk 1:31: Jesus "lifted up" (lit. raised up) Simon's mother-in-law from her bed, and "the fever left her" (cf. also Mk 9:27; Acts 3:7). Of course, for James as for Jesus, there is a relation between the healing of the sick and the final salvation at the coming of the glorious Kingdom of God. In the Jewish mind sickness was associated with sin and with the power of evil. Jesus' miracles of healing were a sign that the Reign of God and the saving power of God overcoming the power of evil were present and active in his ministry. The healing of the sick through the prayer and anointing of the ministers of the church witnesses to the abiding presence and redeeming activity of the Risen Lord and Savior in and through the church. James expresses this relation of the physical healing and the final salvation by adding that if the sick person "has committed sins, he will be forgiven." The prayer and anointing of the church's ministers brings physical and spiritual healing. Perhaps Lev 14:10-31 in which the anointing of lepers with oil is joined to the forgiveness of sins may have influenced the rite of anointing which James recommends.

The Council of Trent declared that the anointing of the sick (which the Reformers had repudiated) was instituted by Christ as a true and proper sacrament and was promulgated by James. Reference is made in the Council's decree to Mk 6:13 which tells us that the Apostles during their missionary tour "cast out many demons and anointed with oil many that were sick and healed them." Nowhere in the

New Testament is there any saying of Jesus commanding the apostles to anoint the sick with oil. Mk 6:7 says that Jesus "began to send them out two by two, and gave them authority over the unclean spirits." Mt 10:1 specifies this authority, "to cast them out, and to heal every disease and infirmity." Both evangelists in their narratives of the apostles' mission during Jesus' ministry are thinking also of the apostolic mission given to the church by the Risen Lord. The anointing of the sick with oil in Mt 6:13 very probably owes its origin to the anointing of the sick practiced in the church for which Mark wrote his gospel, i.e., in the opinion of most New Testament scholars, the Roman church. The manner in which James speaks of the anointing of the sick suggests that it was a rite well-known to his readers. The origin of the rite was very probably the adoption by the early Christian communities of the rabbinical practice of praying over the sick. Institution by Christ our Lord does not mean necessarily that Jesus during his earthly ministry, nor even after his resurrection, instructed the apostles to anoint the sick. The church herself is the sacrament of the Risen Lord, his Body on earth. He has given the church his Spirit enabling and obliging her to channel the graces of his redemption to mankind. When the Church establishes liturgical rites for the dispensation of the healing graces of Christ the Redeemer she acts by reason of the commission and power given by her Lord. In this sense Christ the Lord is the author of the sacrament of the anointing of the sick. "By the sacred anointing of the sick and the prayer of her priests, the whole church commends those who are ill to the suffering and glorified Lord, asking that he may lighten their suffering and save them (cf. Jas 5:14-16). She exhorts them, moreover, to contribute to the welfare of the whole People of God by associating themselves freely with the Passion and death of Christ (cf. Rom 8:17; Col 1:24; 2 Tim 2:11-12; 1 Pt 4:13)." (Vatican II, *Dogmatic Constitution on the Church*, Ch. II, art. 11).

The conjunction "therefore" and the phrase "that you may be healed" connect the exhortation of verses 16-18 to the preceding counsel concerning the anointing of the sick. In the past many Catholic theologians and commentators interpreted verse 16 as a reference to sacramental confession; e.g. St. Thomas Aquinas, (*S. Th. Supl.* q.6, art 6); St. Robert Bellarmine, (*De poenitentia*), Ruch (*Dict. Theol. Cath.* t.V,c 1907-9). Cardinal Cajetan, the 16th century theologian, commentator on St. Thomas' *Summa Theologiae* and exegete, rejected this opinion: "This verse does not treat of sacramental confession as is evident from the phrase 'confess your sins to one another'; sacramental confession is not made to one another but only to priests. The text speaks of that confession by which we acknowledge that we are sinners in need of prayers and which aims at mutual forgiveness and reconciliation" (*Com. in Jac.*). St. Augustine had interpreted the verse in the same way and St. Ven. Bede speaks of a pious custom. Today all commentators, catholic as well as protestant, understand the text in this way. Probably James has in mind the general confession of sinfulness made by the community assembled for worship. The Didache, a Jewish-Christian writing (ca. 80-110 A.D.) contains a similar instruction. "You shall confess your offences in church, and shall not come forward to your prayer with a bad conscience" (Did 4:14), "And on the Lord's Day, after you have come together, break bread and offer the Eucharist, having first confessed your offences, so that your sacrifice may be pure. But let no one who has a quarrel with his neighbor join you until he is reconciled, lest your sacrifice be defiled" (Did 14:1-2). The penitential rite of today's liturgy continues this ancient christian practice. In this context "the healing" can only mean a spiritual healing, i.e. forgiveness of sin and reconciliation with one another. This exhortation to prayer for one another concludes with a maxim which the author confirms and illustrates by a biblical example. "The prayer of a righteous man has great power in its effects" (cf. Prov 15:29). A righteous man (a just man) means in Jas, as it does in Judaism and in Mt, a person who does the will of God, who obeys God's commandments. In support of the axiom that the prayer of the righteous is heard James adduces the example of Elijah, the Prophet. The incident referred to is narrated in 1 Kgs 17-18. The biblical narrative, however, says nothing about the cessation of the rain in response to the prophet's prayer nor does it mention the duration of the drought. James (as also Lk 4:25) apparently depends on a rabbinic story based on the Old Testament narrative. The praise of Elijah in his favorite Old Testament book Sirach 48:2-3 probably suggested this example to James.

The Epistle which is throughout an exhortation to live according to the royal law, i.e. the christian commandment of love, concludes very appropriately with an earnest appeal to labor with loving zeal for the conversion of the brother/sister who has strayed from the truth. We are reminded of Mt's use of Jesus' Parable of the Lost Sheep (Mt 18:10-17). "The truth," as in Jas 1:18 and 3:14, is the gospel, which is called also the royal law because it embraces ethical as well as doctrinal truth. The Christian must not only believe, he must also "do the truth" (Jn 3:21) and "walk in the truth" (3 Jn 3:4).

Those who stray from the truth are first of all, in the context of the epistle, christians who have succumbed to the seductive persuasion of the false teachers. But the expression is applicable also to every Christian who through serious sin has jeopardized his eternal salvation. "Death" in verse 20 means "eternal death," i.e. eternal punishment, as in 1:15. The future tense of the verbs "will save" and "will cover" point to events which will be manifested on the Day of Judgment. There is no doubt that the soul saved from death through fraternal zeal is the sinner who is brought back to the truth. "To cover sins" is a biblical metaphor for the forgiveness of sins similar to the expression "blot out sins" (cf. Ps 32:1; Rom 4:7; Ps 51:1). The subject of "will cover" is the christian who brings back the erring brother/sister to the fold. Does James mean that his loving zeal will win him forgiveness of his own sins? Or does "the multitude of sins" refer to the erring Christian's burden of guilt which is removed at his conversion? A number of ancient commentators, and a few moderns, following Origen, favor the first interpretation. The zealous christian wins through his fraternal love forgiveness of his own sins. This interpretation is probable; James may have had in mind the text of Ezek 3:20-21: "If a righteous man turns from his righteousness and commits iniquity, and I lay a stumbling block before him, he shall die; because you have not warned him he shall die for his sin, and his righteous deeds which he has done shall not be remembered; but his blood I will require at your hand. Nevertheless, if you warn the righteous man not to sin, and he does not sin, he shall surely live, because he took warning; and you will have saved your life." A similar teaching is given by the Pastor in 1 Tim 4:16: "Take heed to yourself and to your teaching; hold to that, for by so doing you will save both yourself and your hearers."

Many commentators understand the "multitude of sins" to refer only to the offenses of the converted sinner. Some interpreters, following St. Ven. Bede, understand the phrase to mean the sins of both the agent of the conversion and of the converted christian. An attractive interpretation of this ambiguous passage is offered by Bo Reicke in the Anchor Bible, Vol. 37, The Epistles of James, Peter and Jude, pp. 62-63: "It might appear that the expression 'covers a multitude of sins' refers to the sins of the individual who rescues an erring brother. But this is not likely in view of the emphasis placed on the multitude of sins in the community. Close study of the context suggests a more appropriate interpretation: the reference is to the erring persons and their community, so that the salvation of those who err prevents the perpetration of numerous sins in society." Reicke finds the source of James' statement in Prov 10:12: "Hatred stirs up strife but love covers all offenses." He gives the same interpretation to 1 Pt 4:8: "Above all hold unfailing your love for one another, since love covers a multitude of sins."

James, who throughout his epistle has warned his readers of the just judgment to come, concludes with an appeal for apostolic love. Christians should emulate the love of Jesus who came not to condemn but to save sinners. It is not the will of their Father in heaven "that one of these little ones should perish." Like the good shepherd those who believe in Jesus, the Savior, should seek out their erring brothers and sisters (cf. Mt 18:10-17).

CONCLUSION

The history of Christianity shows that, from the earliest days of the church down through the centuries to the present, two opposing attitudes have threatened the truth of the gospel. The judaizers, and the antinomians of Corinth were early representatives of these movements. They have reappeared again and again throughout the centuries of the church's history and are present even today. Legalism, with its emphasis on human freedom and responsibility, would make man, in the final analysis, his own redeemer. By his own good works man would literally earn his salvation. Through his obedience to the divine law man would make God his debtor. This attitude was vigorously repudiated by St. Paul in his polemic against the judaizers, and by St. Augustine in his refutation of the Pelagians.

Antinomianism turns Christian liberty into license. Today moral permissiveness is so prevalent, even among professing Christians, that we need James' insistence on the necessity of good works, of the observance of the law of liberty. Christians must not only believe in the gospel; they must live according to the gospel. The word of God speaks to us in James' letter as well as in the Pauline letters. We must hear and heed both.

The Letter of Jude

AN INTRODUCTION
TO JUDE

ORIGEN, THE GREAT Alexandrian biblical and indeed encyclopedic scholar of the third century A.D., wrote of the Epistle of Jude: "Jude wrote a short letter, but one filled with powerful words of heavenly grace" (*In Mt* X, 17). This little letter is a fervid appeal to Christians to hold fast to the faith, i.e. to the doctrinal and moral teaching "which was once for all delivered to the saints" (Jude 3). Most of the Epistle, verses 4 to 16, threatens severe divine punishment on the wicked teachers within the Christian communities who were advocating libertinism and who rejected the sovereignty of Christ.

Our earliest evidence for the existence of the Epistle of Jude is the Second Epistle of Peter. There is certainly a relationship of dependence between Jude and 2 Pt. In the opinion of the vast majority of New Testament scholars, 2 Pt copied Jude. Nineteen of the twenty-five verses of Jude are found in 2 Pt and frequently there is a verbal identity. The description of the false teachers in the second chapter of 2 Pt is based on Jude 4-16. The false teachers deny the lordship of Christ and lead licentious lives (2 Pt 2:1-2 – Jude 4); they despise and revile the good angelic powers (2 Pt 2:10-11 – Jude 8-9); they are loud-mouthed boasters (2 Pt 2:18 – Jude 16); they are blots and blemishes on the Christian love-feasts (2 Pt 2:13 – Jude 12); they are waterless clouds, driven by the wind, for whom the nether gloom of darkness has been reserved forever (2 Pt 2:17 – Jude 12-13). Second Peter's omissions of Jude's use of the Jewish legend about Michael's dispute with the devil (cf. Jude 9 and 2 Pt 2:11); of his allusion to the sexual nature of the sin of the fallen angels (cf. Jude 6 and 2 Pt 2:4); and of his explicit citation of the apocryphal Book of Enoch (Jude 14-15), all point to the priority of Jude. The author of 2 Pt purged Jude's letter of the borrowings from apocryphal Jewish writings which might offend or appear scabrous to his readers. Second Peter, the latest of all the New Testament books, was written during the first half of the second century, probably between 120-140 A.D. Jude, therefore, can not be dated later than toward the turn of the first century, ca. 90-110 A.D.

By the year 200 A.D. the Epistle of Jude was regarded almost everywhere in Christendom as an inspired biblical writing. The Muratorian fragment lists the books of the New Testament canon of the Roman Church toward the end of the second century. It contains only three of the "Catholic" epistles, namely Jude and First and Second John. The churches of Alexandria, of North Africa, in fact all the churches, except the Syrian, regarded Jude as sacred scripture. The church historian Eusebius lists Jude among "the disputed books." St. Jerome recognized the biblical authority of Jude, but he noted that some had doubts and reservations about its canonicity. He wrote: "Jude, the brother of James, has left indeed a little epistle which is one of the seven catholic epistles, but because he appeals in it to the testimony of the book of Enoch, which is apocryphal, it is rejected by some. However, because of its antiquity and use, it merits authority and is numbered among the sacred writings" (*De vir. ill.* IV. P. L. XXI, 374). Since the fourth century the biblical status of Jude has been uncontested. Luther did not consider it one of "the true undoubted principal books of the New Testament." But very few followed him in his desire to expel it from the canon and he bowed to tradition. In 1546 A.D. the Council of Trent solemnly defined the canonicity of the Epistle of Jude.

JUDE'S USE OF APOCRYPHAL WRITINGS.

"In Catholic parlance, the term 'apocrypha' has come to designate ancient Jewish or Christian books from the biblical period (or pretending to be from the biblical period) that have not been accepted as genuine Scripture by the Church" (R.E. Brown, "Apocrypha," J.B.C. 68.6). Pseudonymity is a frequent characteristic of these writings and many of them belong to the literary genre called apocalyptic.

In verses 14-15 Jude cites a passage from the apocryphal Book of Enoch just as he would a biblical passage. No less certain, though less obvious, are the allusions to Enoch in verse 6 and in the phrase about the wandering stars in verse 13 (cf. En 1:9; 40:8; 12:4; 54:3-5). Jude certainly knew well the Book of Enoch and held it in high regard, indeed as a sacred writing. There is also an indubitable allusion to the apocryphal Assumption of Moses in Jude 9, namely the legend about Michael's dispute with the devil over the corpse of Moses. Immediately after the citation from the Book of Enoch (16) Jude describes the wicked teachers as "grumblers," "following their own passions," "loud-mouthed boasters, flattering people to gain advantage." These expressions probably were taken from The Assumption of Moses which, according to the Latin fragment of that writing discovered in Milan in 1861, described with similar phrases a group of men who would assume power over God's people.

St. Jerome tells us that it was Jude's use of apocryphal writings which occasioned doubts and reservations about the biblical authority of the epistle and led some, especially the Syrian Church, to exclude it from the New Testament canon. Even today, there are Christians who feel uneasy with the presence of Jude among the sacred scriptures. They have difficulty reconciling Jude's use of apocryphal writings with their concept of biblical inspiration and truth.

We know that some apocryphal writings, in particular the Book of Enoch, were popular with the Jews and early Christians and highly esteemed by them. Paul, in his beautiful typological interpretation of God's dealings with Israel during the wandering in the Sinai desert, uses the Rabbinic legend about the wandering rock which had become a source of living water when Moses struck it: "the Rock which followed them" (1 Cor 10:4). The Second Epistle to Timothy likens the evil men who will propogate, and, in fact, are propagating their immoral teaching, to "Jannes and Jambres" who "opposed Moses." The Book of Exodus does not name any of the magicians who contested with Moses and Aaron. The names "Jannes and Jambres" originated in Jewish tradition. The Zadokite document called also The Damascus Covenant, a writing very similar to The Manual of Discipline of the Qumran sectaries, speaks of "Jannes and his brother" who were instigated by Beliah to oppose Moses and Aaron (CD 5:19). James expressly designates as scripture the citation from an apocryphal writing which he adduces as a proof in Jas 4:5. We must remember that the Jews had no closed canon of sacred scripture until late in the second century A.D. Until then many Jews, and Christians too, highly esteemed, and regarded as scripture, writings that were not included in the later restricted Jewish canon of the Old Testament. Some of these books which were excluded from the Jewish canon, namely Sirach, Wisdom, Baruch, Judith, Tobit, 1 and 2 Maccabees and the Greek additions to Daniel and Esther, were included in the Christian canon of the Old Testament which was closed by the year 400 A.D. Even after that date some of the apocryphal writings continued to be popular with some Christians. Jude used stories from the apocryphal writings to illustrate the divine judgment and punishment with which he threatens the wicked, licentious teachers who are perverting the Christian communities. Just as a preacher, or religion teacher, who illustrates a doctrinal or moral truth by examples drawn from legends about the saints or from folk history can not reasonably be accused of falsehood, even though he personally may think the stories are true (e.g. The Little Flowers of St. Francis, the story about George Washington and the cherry tree), so neither is Jude's use of apocryphal writings incompatible with biblical inspiration and truth.

THE GREETING.
1-2.

> **1**   Jude, a servant of Jesus Christ and brother of James, To those who are called, beloved in God the Father and kept for Jesus Christ:
> **2**   May mercy, peace, and love be multiplied to you.

The author of this little epistle describes himself as a servant of Jesus Christ and brother of James. Early Christian writers, indeed all commentators, ancient, medieval, and modern, identify this brother of James with the Judas mentioned in the gospels as one of the four brothers of Jesus. "Are not his brothers James and Joseph and Simon and Judas?" (Mt 13:55; cf. Mk 6:3). Why does the author not call himself "brother" of Jesus Christ? The usual answer is because of his deep humility. Of course, in calling himself brother of James he implicitly points to his relationship to Jesus. There is no doubt that he describes himself as brother of James because of the high regard his readers had for James the leader of the Jerusalem Church who was martyred in 62-63 A.D. Jude, and also his addressees, may have known the epistle of James. So the author may be appealing implicitly to that writing in support of his own

severe condemnation of the evil teachers who have infiltrated the Christian communities. There are a few similarities
in the false teachings condemned by both epistles; e.g.
partiality (Jude 16; Jas 2:1-5); antinomianism (Jude 4,8;
Jas 2:14-16). Like Jas 1:1 Jude describes himself as a servant
of Jesus Christ and calls his readers "beloved" (Jude 3,17,20;
Jas 1:16,19; 2:5).

Sts. Jerome and Augustine held that Jude, like his
brother James, was one of the twelve apostles. They identified him with the "Jude of James" in the Lucan lists of
the twelve (Lk 6:16; Acts 1:13) and with the Thaddaeus in
the lists of Mk 3:18 and Mt 10:3. This identification which
has been traditional in Western Christendom is quite
improbable. The New Testament, as was noted in the commentary on James 1:1, clearly distinguishes the twelve
apostles from the Lord's brothers. Moreover, the Lucan
expression "Judas of James" normally means Judas the son
of James. (Recently E. Ellis suggested that "brother of
James" be understood not of blood relationship but in the
meaning "brother" frequently has in the Pauline letters,
namely "helper" or "fellow-worker" in the preaching
of the gospel. Ellis would identify the author of Jude with
the Judas of Acts 15:27. ("Prophecy and Hermeneutic in
Jude," pp. 226-228 in *Prophecy and Hermeneutic in Early
Christianity*, New Testament Essays, Wm. B. Eerdmans
Publ. Co., Grand Rapids, Mich. 1978.)

JUDE IS A PSEUDONYMOUS WRITING

The opinion of St. Jerome that the author of Jude was
the apostle Jude Thaddaeus, the brother of the apostle
James of Alphaeus and relative of Jesus became traditional
in the west. Today it is almost universally held that the
author of Jude is not the apostle Jude Thaddaeus. While
Catholic commentators have tended to defend the authenticity of the epistle, (it was written by Jude, the brother
of James and relative of Jesus), most Protestant scholars

and a few but increasing number of Catholics maintain that Jude is a pseudonymous writing. The arguments in favor of pseudonymity are impressive: 1) The author of this little epistle had an excellent command of the Greek language. His rich vocabulary and syntactical style indicate that Greek was his mother tongue. His excellent use of conjunctions and of participial phrases is thoroughly Greek. Alliterations give a pleasing rhythm to his language. It should also be noted that Jude's citation of Enoch (vv. 14-15) is taken from the Greek version of that book. Jude expresses his thoughts with remarkable vigor, in language that is vivid and powerful. This excellent Greek fits poorly a Jewish Galilean peasant from the obscure village of Nazareth as Jude, the brother of James and relative of Jesus, must have been. Catholic commentators, and the few Protestants, who still maintain the authenticity of the epistle endeavor to escape the force of this argument by postulating that Jude employed a secretary well versed in Greek to write his letter.

2) Verse 17, "But you must remember, beloved, the prediction of the apostles of our Lord Jesus Christ," seems to indicate that the readers, and the author, of the epistle belonged to the second generation of Christians. Jude, brother of James and of Jesus, was a contemporary of Jesus and the apostles.

3) The description of the false teachers condemned in the epistle also points to a time later than the apostolic generation. Their denial of the lordship of Christ and their licentiousness seem to indicate some form of gnosticism, an esoteric movement that began to infiltrate Christianity during the second half of the first century and which eventually evolved into the developed gnostic sects which plagued the church during the second and third centuries. The adherents of this movement pretended to possess an esoteric knowledge (*gnosis*) which made them superior to other christians. Their exaggerated dualism led them to consider all matter evil. As a consequence, they came to

deny the Christian doctrine of the Incarnation and reduced the Son to one among many emanations from the divinity. Their denial of the goodness of matter also led either to an exaggerated asceticism or to complete moral license, to outright licentiousness. The Corinthian church was already infected by this vicious movement when Paul wrote First Corinthians. The apostle condemns the antinomianism and the pretension of some self-styled pneumatics (charismatics) to a "wisdom" not shared by their Christian brothers and sisters. The false teachers of the Epistle to the Colossians, which is perhaps later than Paul (Col 2:8-23), threaten the unique mediatorship of Jesus Christ, promote an exaggerated cult of angelic intermediaries, and manifest the exaggerated asceticism characteristic of some gnostics. The antinomians who were disturbing the churches to which James wrote resemble the wicked teachers condemned by Jude. Second Peter's use of Jude is further evidence for the vitality and growth of this developing gnostic movement. Jude's statement that the wicked teachers deny the sovereignty of our only Lord, Jesus Christ, points to a stage of the movement later than that of 1 Cor.

It would seem, then, that Jude is a pseudonymous writing. The unknown author was a Christian of the hellenistic world who possessed an excellent knowledge of his mother language, Greek. His use of Jewish apocryphal writings would seem to point to a Jewish-Christian born and educated in the Diaspora, i.e. in the Greek-speaking hellenistic world.

THE ADDRESSEES

The addressees of Jude are Christians. They have been called by God and are beloved by their heavenly Father. Faith is man's response to a divine call. God takes the initiative; he chooses and calls. We are reminded of Jesus' words in Jn 6:44: "No one can come to me unless the Father who sent me draws him." The faithful are God's elect and beloved. These titles given to ancient Israel (Dt 32:15; 33:5,26; Is 44:2) now belong to Christians who are "the Israel of God" (Gal 5:16). The expression "called, beloved, *in* God the Father" is difficult. Many copyists obviated the difficulty by changing "beloved" (*egapemenous*) to "sanctified" (*egiasmenous*): the faithful have been sanctified in God the Father. But the reading in (*en*) is supported by the most authoritative and ancient manuscripts. The preposition in (*en*) can be and is used, even though infrequently, to designate the agent of an action. Jude's expression is the equivalent of Paul's "beloved by God" in 1 Thess 1:4.

Jude's readers have also been kept or guarded by God the Father for Jesus Christ. Perhaps Jude distinguishes the Christians to whom he is writing from those who had also been called but had succumbed to the seduction of the wicked teachers whom he is going to condemn. God the Father has kept and is keeping Jude's readers faithful to their call and finally for participation in the glory of Jesus Christ. In Jn 17:11 Jesus prays: "Holy Father keep them in thy name, which thou hast given me, that they may be one, even as we are one." The perfect Greek participles, beloved and kept, indicate a past divine action which perdures in the present.

Jude concludes his greeting with a prayer that his readers may share in ever greater measure God's merciful forgiveness and love and the peace which Jesus promised to his disciples (Jn 14:17), namely, that peace which sums up and contains all the blessings of God's redemption in and through Christ. The passive verb in a prayer implies that the blessings desired are God's gifts. 1 Pt 1:2; 2 Pt 1:2; 2 Jn 3 have similar greeting prayers.

Were the churches addressed by Jude Jewish-Christian communities or Gentile churches? Scholars are sharply divided. Jude's use of apocryphal Jewish writings would seem to indicate Jewish-Christian readers. But the libertinism and licentiousness promoted by the false teachers would point to Christians from a pagan background. We can be reasonably certain that the readers of Jude were Christians living in the Greek-speaking hellenistic world. The churches they belonged to probably included Christians of Jewish background and many of gentile origin. We simply do not know the region of the hellenistic world where these Christians lived. A number of commentators suggest Syria. But that is pure conjecture. Perhaps the unknown author of the epistle placed his writing under the aegis of Jude, the brother of James, because he was writing to the same churches to which James sent his letter. This guess is as good as any. But it does not tell us where Jude's addressees lived because we do not know where James' readers dwelt.

Jude was written after the Epistle of James and before Second Peter; probably toward the turn of the first century, ca. 90-110 A.D.

THE OCCASION AND PURPOSE OF THE EPISTLE. 3-4.

> **3** Beloved, being very eager to write to you of our common salvation, I found it necessary to write appealing to you to contend for the faith which was once for all delivered to the saints.
> **4** For admission has been secretly gained by some who long ago were designated for this condemnation, ungodly persons who pervert the grace of our God into licentiousness and deny our only Master and Lord, Jesus Christ.

Jude was contemplating writing a letter which would treat of "our common salvation," i.e. of the eternal happiness and participation in the glory of Christ to which he and his readers were called and for which they were being guarded by God their loving Father. Then he received alarming news. Evil teachers had infiltrated the Christian communities and were endangering their fidelity to God and Christ. He felt compelled, therefore, to write at once to warn his readers about the danger which threatened them. So he hastily composed this little letter appealing to them to fight for the faith which is the precious heritage they and all their fellow Christians, who have been sanctified in Christ, received. "The faith once for all delivered to the saints" does not signify the act of faith, i.e. the individual's response surrendering himself/herself to God calling and drawing in the proclamation of the gospel. It designates the content of Christian belief, i.e. the doctrinal and moral teaching which was imparted to all those who heeded God's call and were baptized. This faith was already a tradition, a deposit, which must be preserved intact. We are reminded of the Pastor's appeal to Timothy: "Guard what has been entrusted to you. Avoid the godless chatter and contradictions of what is falsely called knowledge, for by professing it some have missed the mark as regards the faith" (1 Tim 16:20-21). Cf. also 2 Thess 2:15; Rom 16:17 and 1 Cor 11:2 where Paul reminds his readers of "the doctrine which you have been taught" and of "the traditions" he has delivered to them. The Christian must fight to preserve this faith. He must struggle against his own self-centeredness, against the powers of evil, and against false teachers (cf. Eph 6:10-17; 1 Pt 5:8,9; 1 Tim 1:18,19; 6:12).

The evil teachers who had infiltrated the communities were professing Christians, probably wandering teachers like those mentioned in 2 Jn 7-10 and in the Didache 11:1-2. But Jude can not bring himself to call them "brothers." In the Greek text he disdainfully introduces them as "certain people," who "have sneaked into" the communities under false pretensions. They are ungodly, i.e. impious persons, "who pervert the grace of our God," i.e. the freedom from sin, the powers of evil, and from the Law, which is God's gift in Christ the redeemer, into an excuse for moral licence. They make Christian liberty a justification for licentiousness. Thus they reject by their evil behavior the sovereignty of Christ. They deny in practice the basic Christian creed,

Jesus Christ is Lord! These false teachers of Jude remind us of the Nicolaitans condemned in the book of Revelation 2:14-15, 20-24, and of the wicked teachers condemned in 2 Pt 2:1-3. Some scholars think that the false teachers espoused the gnostic doctrine which attributed the creation of the material world not to God but to the Demiurge and which made Christ one of the Aeons, an intermediary between God and men (cf. e.g. J. Mayor, *The Epistle of St. Jude and the Second Epistle of St. Peter*). Since nothing more is said of the false teachers' denial of our only Master and Lord, it seems more probable that Jude regards their licentiousness as a practical rejection of Jesus' Lordship. Their conduct is the equivalent of a denial of the Christian creed; cf. Tit 1:16 "They profess to know God, but they deny Him by their deeds"; the false teachers of Jude profess to be Christians but by their immoral lives they reject the sovereignty of Christ. Christian liberty frees the believer from the bondage of sin and selfishness and enables him/her to worship, serve and obey God in and with Christ. St. Ireneus in his classic work usually called *Adversus Haereses*, but which he titled: "Detection and Overthrow of the Pretended but False Gnosis" gives a description of the immorality of some Gnostics of the late second century A.D., which warrants us to place Jude's false teachers within the evolving gnostic movement: "As gold sunk in filth does not lose its beauty but preserves its own nature, the filth being unable to harm the gold, so they say of themselves that even if they be immersed in material deeds, nothing will injure them nor will they lose their spiritual essence. Therefore 'the most perfect' among them do unafraid all the forbidden things of which Scripture tells us that 'they who do such things will not inherit the kingdom of God'" (*Adv. Haer* 1:6; 2-3).

The ungodly false teachers will not escape divine punishment which Jude will illustrate with examples in verses 5-7. In fact, he declares, they were long ago designated (lit. "written about") for this condemnation. The prophecy to

which he alludes is probably the passage of Enoch which
he cites in verses 14-15.

THE IMPENDING PUNISHMENT OF
THE WICKED TEACHERS.
5-7.

> **5** Now I desire to remind you, though you were once
> for all fully informed, that he who saved a people out of
> the land of Egypt, afterward destroyed those who did
> not believe. **6** And the angels that did not keep their
> own position but left their proper dwelling have been
> kept by him in eternal chains in the nether gloom until
> the judgment of the great day; **7** just as Sodom and
> Gomorrah and the surrounding cities, which likewise
> acted immorally and indulged in unnatural lust, serve as
> an example by undergoing a punishment of eternal fire.

Jude supports his exhortation to fight for the faith by
assuring his readers that the ungodly teachers who have
sneaked into their communities will not escape the divine
punishment. He invites them to reflect on three examples
of the divine chastisement which they already know of,
because they have been well instructed. These incidents
illustrate the punishment that threatens the wicked teachers.

The first example is God's punishment of the Hebrews
who climaxed their repeated grumbling against him when
they murmured against Moses and Aaron because they
believed the false evil report of the men who had been sent
to spy out the land of Canaan. None of the people who had
been delivered from Egyptian bondage, except Caleb and
Joshua, would enter into the promised land. "Your dead
bodies shall fall in this wilderness. And your children
shall be shepherds in this wilderness forty years, and shall
suffer for your faithlessness, until the last of your dead
bodies lies in the wilderness" (Num 4:32-33). In both the Old
and the New Testaments this chastisement of rebellious,

ungrateful and unbelieving Israel has become a type of God's punishment of the disobedient and faithless (cf. Ps 95:8-11; Sir 16:9-10; 1 Cor 10:1-11; Heb 3:7-4:11).

Verse 5 of Jude presents a classical and extremely difficult problem of text-criticism. The RSV translation "he who saved," while suggesting the interpretation of most translators and commentators, namely "the Lord," i.e. God, as the subject of the sentence, really does not specify the subject. It has no support in the ancient manuscripts and versions. The RSV acknowledges this in a footnote: "ancient authorities read *Jesus* or *the Lord* or *God*." The editors of RSV apparently accepted the conjecture of the nineteenth century British New Testament scholar, Fenton J. Hort, that the subject of the sentence in the original Greek text was the definite article *ho* employed as a relative pronoun, i.e. "he who." Catholic versions of the New Testament which are translations of the Latin vulgate have Jesus as the subject of the verb saved; e.g. The Douay-Rheims-Challoner Bible, and the Confraternity Revision of it. Catholic English translations of the Greek text, e.g. The Jerusalem Bible and The New American Bible read "the Lord" obviously meaning God. The New English Bible, an interdenominational translation of British scholars, also reads "the Lord." A footnote, however, states: "Some witnesses read *Jesus* (which might be understood as *Joshua*)." While it is true that the hebrew name Joshua is written "Jesus" in Greek, this suggestion of the NEB, which was also made by St. Jerome, is highly improbable in view of the context. In the Greek text the subject of verses 5 and 6 is the same, and Joshua cannot be the subject of verse 6.

The authoritative and ancient Greek manuscripts, the ancient versions, e.g. the latin vulgate, the coptic and ethiopic, as well as the testimony of the great biblical scholars of the third and fourth centuries, Origen and St. Jerome, overwhelmingly support the reading, "Jesus." Consequently several critical editions of The Greek New Testament, most noteworthy the first (1966) and second (1968) edited by an international committee of scholars recognized as the most distinguished and competent in the field of New Testament textual research, and published by the United Societies as a translators' text, read "Jesus." The editors, however, graded this reading D, i.e. very doubtful. The third edition of this monumental work (1975) changed the reading "Jesus" to "the Lord." But again the editors graded their choice D. On behalf of and in cooperation with the editorial committee Bruce M. Metzger, the distinguished American New Testament text-critic, wrote *A Textual Commentary On The Greek New Testament* in which he gives the reasons that led the editors of the third edition to adopt certain variant readings for inclusion in the text and to relegate certain other readings to the apparatus. This companion volume to the third edition was published in 1971, four years before the publication of the third edition of the text itself. Dr. Metzger explains the change from "Jesus" to "the Lord" in Jude 5: "Despite the weighty attestation supporting *Iesous* (Jesus) . . . a majority of the committee was of the opinion that the reading was difficult to the point of impossibility, and explained its origin in terms of transcriptional oversight (KC being taken for IC)" (*op. cit.* p. 725-6). KC is the usual scribal abbreviation for *Kyrios* (Lord); IC the abbreviation for *Iesous* (Jesus). It is also quite probable that the presence of the name Jesus in so many of the early manuscripts and versions may be due to the well-attested Christian desire to attribute to Jesus a role in the events of Old Testament history, especially in the Exodus history which the New Testament views as a type of the redemption accomplished in and through Jesus. 1 Cor 10:4,9 already shows this Christian tendency. St. Justin Martyr, the great lay apologist for christianity (+ ca. 165 A.D.) wrote in his Dialogue with the Jew Trypho: "For all of us who are of the Gentiles are not expecting Judah, but Jesus, who also delivered your forefathers from Egypt" (Dial ch. 120). In spite of the fact that the reading Jesus in Jude 5 is, as Metzger noted, "the best attested reading among Greek and versional witnesses" (*op.*

cit. p. 726) it is excluded by the context. He who saved Israel from Egypt and punished the unfaithful Israelites with death in the desert is also he who punished the fallen angels. The punishment of the angels has never been attributed to Jesus. 2 Pt 2:4 in a passage that is dependent on Jude explicitly attributes the punishment of the sinful angels to God.

Jude presents as his second example of divine punishment the awful chastisement inflicted by God on the sinful angels. The expressions he uses in his very brief description of this punishment indicate that he has in mind the Book of Enoch's embellishment of the story about the fall of the angels in Gen 6:1-4. En 12:4 speaks of the angels "who have abandoned the high heaven and the holy eternal place." Jude says they "did not keep their own position," i.e. the domain, the sphere of influence, assigned them by God or the charge he had given them; "but they left their proper dwelling." In punishment God is keeping them "in eternal chains in the nether gloom until (or better, for) the judgment of the great day." They had lived in the heavens; now they are imprisoned in the darkness of Sheol. And this is not their final punishment! They are being kept for a terrible fate to which they will be sentenced on the day of judgment. En 54:3-5 describes the immense chains prepared for Azazel, one of the leaders of the sinful angels. And in En 18:12 we read: "Bind them . . . until the day of their judgment"; and in En 22:11 "until the great day of judgment."

Jude does not explicitly mention the sin of the fallen angels, but he leaves no doubt that he accepted the Book of Enoch's interpretation of Gen 6:1-2 which was current in Judaism and early Christianity, namely that the fallen angels had committed a horrible sexual sin; they had cohabited with human females. The angels "saw that the daughters of men were fair; and they took to wife such of them as they chose" (Gen 6:2). The Book of Jubilees, The Testaments of the Twelve Patriarchs, the Alexandrian Jewish scholar Philo, some rabbinical texts, and several church Fathers, e.g. St. Cyprian and St. Ambrose all accept this interpretation of Gen 6:1-2. Some manuscripts of the Greek version of the Old Testament which was the Bible of Jude and his readers, render "the sons of God" of the Hebrew text by "the angels" [cf. LXX (Cod. A)]. This is very probably the meaning of the Hebrew text. The expression "sons of God" in the Hebrew bible frequently designates the heavenly beings who belong to the court or the army of God, who serve him and also act as his messengers, i.e. angels (cf. e.g. Ps 29:1; Ps 89:7; Job 38:7). Most modern exegetes regard Gen 6:1-4 as a fragment of an ancient myth which originally described the love affairs of gods with women. In Gen 6:1-4 the gods are changed to angels and the ancient, widespread myth is used to illustrate the moral corruption of humanity which led God to repent that he had created mankind and to send the great flood. Jude's statement that Sodom and Gomorrah, and the surrounding cities which (translating literally) "*in the same way as they*," indulged in immorality and went after "*strange flesh*" is decisive for the conclusion that Jude, as should be expected, shared the opinion of Jews and Christians of his day that the sin of the fallen angels was sexual, cohabitation with women. In the Greek text of Jude, Sodom and Gomorrah are feminine nouns. This is clearly indicated by the feminine pronoun in the phrase "the cities around *them*." The pronoun in the phrase "in the same way as *they*" is masculine. It can only refer back to the masculine noun "the angels." Sodom and Gomorrah and the surrounding cities were destroyed because, like the angels who lusted after and sinned with women, they went after (lit.) "*strange flesh*," i.e. flesh that was not human. The reference is to Gen 19. The inhabitants of Sodom lusted after "the two angels" (Gen 19:1) who in the form of men were given hospitality by Lot. In punishment "the Lord rained on Sodom and Gomorrah brimstone and fire from the Lord out of heaven; and he overthrew those cities, and all the valley, and all the inhabitants of the cities, and what grew on the ground" (Gen 19:24-25). According to the

biblical tradition Sodom and the other cities of the Penta-
polis were situated in the region south of the Dead Sea, a
region that is frightfully desolate. The rain "of brimstone
and fire" and "the smoke of a furnace" (Gen 19:24,28) seem to
indicate a volcanic eruption. The bitumen which rises from
submerged pits to the surface of the shallow southern end
of the Dead Sea, the many sulphur deposits in the region,
the hot springs and the dense vapors led the author of
Wisdom to say that "Evidence of their (Sodom's and the
neighboring cities') wickedness still remains; a continually
smoking wasteland" (Wis 10:7). The destruction of Sodom
and Gomorrah became in the prophetic literature a type
and a frightful example of the punishment of the wicked
(cf. e.g. Amos 4:11; Is 13:19; Jer 23:14). Jude stands in this
prophetic tradition. He declares that they "serve as an
example by undergoing a punishment of eternal fire." The
"lake of fire that burns with brimstone" into which the
beast, the false prophet, the devil, and the condemned
wicked are thrown (Rev 19:20; 20:10) also owes its origin
to this tradition.

Jude shares the ideas about the nature of the angels
which were current in Judaism and early Christianity.
Angels were heavenly beings, but not pure spirits. In both
the Old Testament and the New Testament angels, when
sent to earth, appear in human form (cf. e.g. Gen 19:1; Tob
5:4; 12:15-19; Mk 16:5; Acts 1:10). But their "bodies" were
not human. They had "ethereal" bodies of an entirely
different nature from humans. They are usually depicted
as males and so capable of sexual intercourse with human
females. The book of Jubilees, which was highly esteemed
by the Qumran sectaries and may have been composed by a
Qumran Essene, states that the angels of the Presence, the
superior angels, were created circumcised (Jub 15:27).
Pseudo-Dionysius whose writings can not be dated earlier
than the fifth century A.D. is apparently the first Christian
author to insist on the complete spirituality of the angels.
But his teaching was opposed for centuries because of the

contrary traditional opinion. It was not until St. Thomas Aquinas (cf. *S. Th.* 1, q. 50, *art.* 1) that the complete spirituality of the angelic nature became the accepted and common teaching of Christian theology.

THE ARROGANT BLASPHEMY AND PERVERSITY OF THE FALSE TEACHERS.
8-13.

8 Yet in like manner these men in their dreamings defile the flesh, reject authority, and revile the glorious ones. **9** But when the archangel Michael, contending with the devil, disputed about the body of Moses, he did not presume to pronounce a reviling judgment upon him, but said, "The Lord rebuke you." **10** But these men revile whatever they do not understand, and by those things that they know by instinct as irrational animals do, they are destroyed. **11** Woe to them! For they walk in the way of Cain, and abandon themselves for the sake of gain to Balaam's error, and perish in Korah's rebellion. **12** These are blemishes on your love feasts, as they boldly carouse together, looking after themselves, waterless clouds, carried along by winds; fruitless trees in late autumn, twice dead, uprooted; **13** wild waves of the sea, casting up the foam of their own shame; wandering stars for whom the nether gloom of darkness has been reserved for ever.

The opening phrase of v.8, "Yet in like manner these men," joins this section of the epistle to the preceding verses. The false teachers have learned nothing from history. On the contrary, their arrogance has blinded them to the lessons taught by God's punishment of the wicked. They are dreamers who pay more heed to their pretended visions than they do to God's word. They boast that they possess a knowledge superior to that of the ordinary Christians, but their perverse behavior shows that their pretended revelations are the product of their own corrupt minds and do not come from the Holy Spirit. Jude levels three accusations against "these men." In verse 4 he had accused them of perverting the grace of God into licentiousness. Now he repeats this accusation with emphasis: "in their dreamings they defile the flesh." In v.10 Jude declares that the licentiousness of the evil teachers is the fruit of their erroneous doctrines. This is insinuated in v.8, "in their dreamings" they defile the flesh. In v.10 he writes: "by those things that they know by instinct as irrational animals do, they are destroyed," a literal translation of the Greek text is "they are corrupted." There is no doubt that Jude is referring to the licentiousness of the false teachers. In v.8 they are accused of rejecting authority, and of reviling the glorious ones; in v.10 they "revile whatever they do not understand."

The Greek word *kyriotes* in v.8, translated "authority" by RSV, means literally "sovereignty, lordship." In the epistles to the Colossians and the Ephesians it refers to a special class of angels (cf. Col 1:16; Eph 1:21), a meaning it also has in the Book of Enoch. The commentators are divided in their interpretation of the word in v.8. Some understand "authority" to refer to church authorities. Bo Reicke (*op. cit.* p. 202) maintains that the false teachers are accused of being rebels against the existing order. "Anarchistic and antinomian tendencies must be attributed to them." All the commentators who understand the term to refer to human authorities, ecclesiastical or civil, appeal to v.11 which likens the false teachers to Korah who rebelled against Moses. However, in view of the parallel between v.4 and v.8 it seems more probable that the authority which the wicked teachers reject is the sovereignty, the lordship of Christ. Both the Didache 4:1 and Hermas Similitudes (or Parables) V, vi, 1 attribute *kyriotes*, sovereignty, to Christ ("the Lord" in Did., "the Son of God" in Hermas). The RSV translation, like the Greek text, is ambiguous and patient of any of the proposed interpretations.

The third crime of the false teachers is that they "revile the glorious ones (lit. "the glories"). The following v.9 leaves no doubt that Jude accuses the evil teachers of despising the good angels. The enormity of this arrogant contempt is illustrated by the respect the archangel Michael showed for the angelic nature of the devil, wicked and fallen though he was. Even in the heat of his dispute with the devil over the corpse of Moses, Michael "did not presume to pronounce a reviling judgment upon him, but said, 'The Lord rebuke you.' But these men revile whatever they do not understand."

Clement of Alexandria (+ 215 A.D.), Origen + 253 A.D.), and Didymus (+ 398 A.D.) all note that Jude's story about Michael's dispute with the devil is found in the Jewish apocryphal book The Assumption of Moses. In fact Didymus says that the Manicheans, who did not believe in the fall of the angels, rejected both the Epistle of Jude and the Assumption of Moses precisely because of this story about Michael's dispute with the devil.

But the original hebrew text of the Assumption of Moses and the Greek version have been lost. In 1861 a portion of a latin translation in a sixth century manuscript was discovered in Milan by the librarian of the famous Ambrosian Library. The original book was probably composed between 4 B.C. and 30 A.D. Unfortunately the latin portion which has been discovered does not contain the legend about Michael's dispute with the devil. But from the references to the story in early Christian authors and in several rabbinical writings the essential elements of it can be reconstructed. The following reconstruction depends chiefly on that of M.R. James in The Second Epistle General of Peter and the General Epistle of Jude.

The Book of Deuteronomy briefly records Moses' death and burial. "So Moses the servant of the Lord died there in the land of Moab, according to the word of the Lord, and he buried him in the valley in the land of Moab opposite

Beth-péor; but no man   knows the place of his burial to this day" (Dt 34:5-6). It seems that this ignorance of Moses' burial places lies at the origin of the story of the Assumption of Moses. When Michael and his angels were preparing to bury Moses' corpse, Satan (called Samuel in the rabbinic writings) appeared and said that the body belonged to him because he was the Lord of matter. Michael withstood him, denying his claim. The Acts of the Council of Nicaea contains this reference to the story: "In the book of the Assumption of Moses the archangel Michael, when disputing with the devil, said to him "We have all been created by his (God's) holy Spirit"(Mansi, Vol. II, p. 857). Probably Michael then accused Satan of having marred God's good creation. Origen, citing the Assumption of Moses, writes that the serpent inspired by the devil was the cause of the sin of Adam and Eve (cf. *De Principiis* III, 2:1). Oecumenius, a tenth century Greek commentator, states that the devil declared that Moses was not deserving of burial at all, because he was a murderer (cf. Ex 2:11-14). Probably, as St. Ambrose suggests, Satan wanted to get hold of Moses' body in order to make it an object of idolatrous worship by the Israelites. Michael was angry, but he restrained himself and said in the words of Zech 3:2 "the Lord rebuke you, O Satan!" This behavior of the prince angel Michael shows up the appalling arrogance of the false teachers who despise and revile the good angels.

"Woe to them!" A horrible fate awaits them because they are following the evil example of Cain, Balaam, and Korah. Cain, the murderer of his brother Abel, became in Jewish tradition the prototype of the ungodly wicked who are consumed by jealousy and are self-seeking even in their worship of God. Philo, who regarded Cain as the type of selfish egoism, also considered him to be the exemplar of teachers who oppose God. Some commentators suggest that Jude is accusing the false teachers of spiritual murder; they destroy the soul of their Christian brothers and sisters by their seductive teaching and evil example.

The Book of Numbers presents two different pictures of Balaam, the pagan soothsayer. In one (Num 22:5-7) he is a prophet who, against his own will and desire, is impelled by God to bless Israel. In the other (Num 25:1-5; 31:8,16; Jos 13:22) he induces the Israelites "to play the harlot with the daughters of Moab" and to participate in idolatrous worship. He was killed by Israel in the battle against Midian. It is this second tradition that Jude had in mind when he wrote that the false teachers "abandon themselves for the sake of gain to Balaam's error." Jude insinuates that, like Balaam who was hired by Balak, the false teachers were exploiting the Christian communities, accepting fees for their deceitful teaching. We are reminded of the Nicolaitans who threatened the faith and morality of the churches of the Apocalypse; cf. Rev. 2:14-15, the letter to the church in Pergamum: "But I have a few things against you: you have some there who hold the teaching of Balaam who taught Balak to put a stumbling block before the sons of Israel, that they might eat food sacrificed to idols and practice immorality. So you also have some who hold the teaching of the Nicolaitans."

The evil teachers who reject authority, denying "our only Master and Lord Jesus Christ," will be punished as were Korah and his followers who rebelled against Moses and Aaron. The earth opened and swallowed them up and they went down alive into Sheol. Thus Israel knew "that these men have despised the Lord" (Num 16).

Jude continues his scathing censure of the evil teachers with metaphors taken from nature and from the popular association of angels with stars. They presume to participate in the Christian love-feasts which they soil by their conduct, because they carouse together concerned only with satisfying their own gluttony. This is the interpretation of RSV which renders the Greek word *spilades* (sing. *spilas*) by "blemishes." This is a possible interpretation and it is given by many commentators. They appeal to the parallel passage of 2 Pt 2:13 which changes the *spilades* of Jude to *spiloi*, which in the Greek of the New Testament period meant "spots," or "stains": cf. the metaphorical use of the word in Eph 5:27. *Spilas*, the word employed by Jude, means a rock washed by the sea, a hidden reef. (The margin of RSV gives "reefs" as an alternative translation.) A number of scholars insist on the translation "reefs," because that is the usual and primary meaning of the Greek word and is better suited to the context which describes the teachers with metaphors drawn from nature. Hidden, submerged reefs are a dangerous threat to the safety of ships. By their presence in the love-feasts of the Christians the evil teachers are a scandal to the faithful, threatening them with spiritual shipwreck. The JB translation expresses this interpretation nicely: "They are a dangerous obstacle to your community meals, coming for the food and quite shamelessly only looking after themselves."

The "love-feasts" were the Christian community meals which in the early church, in some places even beyond the first century, accompanied the celebration of the Eucharist. Jude is the first Christian writer to employ the Greek word *agape*, love, as the name of the community meal. It emphasizes the dispositions with which the Christians should participate in the fraternal celebration. Ignatius of Antioch, who was martyred early in the second century, ca. 110-117 A.D., quite clearly employs *agape* for the Eucharist. He writes in his letter to the Smyrnaeans VIII.2: "Wherever the bishop appears let the congregation be present; just as wherever Jesus Christ is, there is the Catholic Church. It is not lawful either to baptise or to hold an 'agape' without the bishop; but whatever he approves, this is also pleasing to God, that everything you do may be secure and valid." His reference to "incorruptible love" in his letter to the Romans also has a eucharistic connotation. "I have no pleasure in the food of corruption or in the delights of this life. I desire 'the bread of God,' which is the flesh of Jesus Christ, who was 'of the seed of David,' and for drink I desire his blood, which is incorruptible love *(agape)*". The earliest extant Christian

writing which treats of the Eucharist is Paul's First Epistle
to the Corinthians. He calls it "The Lord's Supper"; it is a
fraternal meal in the course of which, probably at the end,
the Eucharist is celebrated (cf. 1 Cor 11:17-29). The behavior of the false teachers whom Jude condemns reminds
us of the abuses in the celebration of the Lord's Supper
which Paul condemned in 1 Cor. Instead of sharing with
their poor brothers and sisters the food and drink they had
brought for the fraternal meal, some of the better-off
Christians feasted together, eating and drinking to excess.
In the language of Paul these selfish gluttons were "guilty
of profaning the body and blood of the Lord." Jude accuses
the evil teachers of a similar behavior: "they boldly carouse
together, looking after themselves," literally "pasturing,"
or "feeding themselves." Perhaps by his use of the word
which properly signifies the action of a shepherd leading
sheep to pasture, Jude is hinting that the false teachers who
have won admittance into the Christian communities under
the pretense of imparting a profound spiritual doctrine
are like the leaders of Israel whom Ezekiel condemned: "Ho
shepherds of Israel who have been feeding yourselves! Should
not shepherds feed the sheep?" (Ezek 34:2; cf. also Jn
10:1-2, 9-10).

Like waterless clouds and barren fruit trees the false
teachers are not only worthless but deceitful; they promise
to edify the communities, but they corrupt them. Like waves
casting up all sorts of filth from the depths of the sea they
pervert the grace of God into licentiousness. The fate of the
fallen angels (wandering stars) will be theirs; eternal
punishment in the nether gloom of darkness.

The ancient Greeks believed the stars to be living beings,
indeed gods. This belief was also shared by other ancient
peoples. In the Old Testament the stars are ministers of
God. They receive and execute his commands, and they
proclaim his glory (cf. Is 45:12; Ps 148:1-3). They are
associated with angels. In the Old Testament God is frequently called Yahweh Sabaoth, i.e. Lord of hosts, namely

of the stars, the heavenly armies. In the Apocalypse of
Isaiah (ch. 24-27 of the Book of Isaiah) we read that on the
great day of judgment God will punish the rebellious stars,
i.e. the sinful angels, "They will be gathered together as
prisoners in a pit; they will be shut up in a prison, and after
many days they will be punished" (cf. Is 24:21-22). The
Book of Enoch contains many references to the star-angels
and speaks of the punishment of the sinful angels, "the
wandering stars" (cf. En 18:13-16; 21:2-6). In the Apocalypse of John the star Wormwood which fell from heaven
like a burning torch and poisoned a third of the waters is
an evil angel, as is also the fallen star of Rev 9:1-2 (cf. Rev
8:10-11). Jude undoubtedly is alluding to the Book of
Enoch. The false teachers, he declares, will be punished
like the fallen angels.

THE PROPHECY OF ENOCH.
14-16.

> **14** It was of these also that Enoch in the seventh
> generation from Adam prophesied, saying, "Behold, the
> Lord came with his holy myriads, **15** to execute judg-
> ment on all, and to convict all the ungodly of all their
> deeds of ungodliness which they have committed in such
> an ungodly way, and of all the harsh things which un-
> godly sinners have spoken against him." **16**   These are
> grumblers, malcontents, following their own passions,
> loud-mouthed boasters, flattering people to gain
> advantage.

Jude concluded his invective against the false teachers
with the declaration that they would be punished as were
the fallen angels. Now he declares that their chastisement
had been predicted long ago by the patriarch Enoch. The
prophecy which he quotes from the book of Enoch embraces the false teachers as well as the ungodly of antiquity.
The Book of Enoch is, of course, a pseudonymous writing.

In fact it is a collection of writings by a number of authors, rather than a book, the product of one author. For centuries the book, which was written in Aramaic, was known only from an Ethiopic translation of a Greek version, and from some fragments of the Greek and latin versions. Today we possess ten fragments of the Aramaic text which were found among the Dead Sea Scrolls. This discovery testifies to the high esteem in which the work was held by the Qumran sectaries. The original writing dates from the Maccabean period, perhaps shortly after the Book of Daniel. Just as the author of Daniel writing ca. 165 B.C. presents his work as the prophecy of a sixth century B.C. Jewish exile in Babylonia named Daniel, so the author of Enoch writes in the name of the antediluvian patriarch Enoch, the seventh from Adam (cf. Gn 5:3-18; 1 Chron 1:1-3). Enoch who is described in the book of Genesis as a man "who walked with God" was highly esteemed in Judaism, and the verses with which Genesis concludes its account of his life gave rise to many legends. "Thus all the days of Enoch were three hundred and sixty-five years. Enoch walked with God; and he was not, for God took him" (Gen 5:23-24). This was taken to mean that the patriarch did not die, but that he was assumed alive into heaven. Thus we read in the Book of Sirach: "No one like Enoch has been created on earth, for he was taken up from the earth" (Sir 49:14). According to the Book of Jubilees (4:23) he was taken to the Garden of Eden. The Epistle to the Hebrews also speaks of Enoch's assumption. "By faith Enoch was taken up so that he should not see death; and he was not found, because God had taken him. Now before he was taken he was attested as having pleased God" (Heb 11:5). Jude's use of the Book of Enoch which he cites as sacred scripture reflects the veneration in which the ancient patriarch and the writing attributed to him were held in early Christianity. Many Christians revered the Book of Enoch as sacred scripture. In fact when the church was drawing up her canon of the Old Testament there were a number of Christians who wanted the Book of Enoch included in the sacred collection. Origen notes that several churches held the writing to be a sacred book. Jude cites En 1:9 from the Greek version of the book. The passage is a typical apocalyptic description of the final judgment (cf. e.g. Zech 14:5; Mt 16:27; 25:31).

The expression in the prophecy "of all the harsh things which ungodly sinners have spoken against him (i.e. God)," prompts Jude to level another accusation against the false teachers. The phrases with which he expresses his accusation were probably taken from the Assumption of Moses (VII. 7, 9 and V. 5). The false teachers grumble against God complaining of their lot because they esteem themselves superior to others. They are loud-mouthed boasters who follow their own passions and obsequiously flatter those who they think may be able to further their selfish interests.

EXHORTATIONS TO THE FAITHFUL.
17-23.

17 But you must remember, beloved, the predictions of the apostles of our Lord Jesus Christ; **18** they said to you, "In the last time there will be scoffers, following their own ungodly passions." **19** It is these who set up divisions, worldly people, devoid of the Spirit. **20** But you, beloved, build yourselves up on your most holy faith; pray in the Holy Spirit; **21** keep yourselves in the love of God; wait for the mercy of our Lord Jesus Christ unto eternal life. **22** And convince some, who doubt; **23** save some, by snatching them out of the fire; on some have mercy with fear, hating even the garment spotted by the flesh.

At the beginning of verse 5 Jude addressed the faithful, "Now I desire to remind you," but from then on until the end of v.16 he focused his attention on the evil teachers, on the punishment that awaited those deceitful men, on their immorality and arrogant contempt of the angels, indeed even of Christ the Lord! He described them as intruders into the Christian communities, who were endangering the salvation of the faithful, and he concluded with Enoch's prophecy of the horrible sentence they would receive on judgment day. Now, in v.17-23, he turns to the faithful themselves to reassure them and to exhort them to persevere in their christian commitment. They should not be dismayed and frightened because of the evil teachers who have infiltrated their communities. The activity of such scoffers is one of the trials of the last days in which christians are living. By steadfast perseverance in the faith, by prayer in the Holy Spirit, they will continue to abide in the love of God while they look forward with confident hope to receive a merciful judgment from the Lord Jesus Christ which will bring them into eternal life.

V.17, "But you must remember, beloved, the predictions of the apostles of our Lord Jesus Christ," quite clearly indicates that the author of the epistle did not belong to the apostolic body or to their generation. The imperfect tense of the verb in the opening phrase of v.18, (lit.) "how they used to tell you," or "how they kept on telling you," implies that the apostolic predictions about the end time were a prominent feature of the religious instruction of the christian communities; cf. e.g. Acts 20:29-31 (Paul's exhortation to the elders of Ephesus): "I know that after my departure fierce wolves will come in among you, not sparing the flock; and from among your own selves will arise men speaking perverse things, to draw away the disciples after them"; also 2 Tim 3:1-5; 4:3-4; 2 Pt 3:3. These predictions are an echo of Jesus' saying about the false prophets who would attempt to seduce the faithful before his parousia (cf. Mk 13:22; Mt 24:24).

The expression "in the last time" is the equivalent of "in the last days" of Acts 2:17 and Heb 1:2. The final period of salvation history dawned with the coming of Christ. In the sermon of Acts 2:17-36 Peter declares that the Lord's resurrection and gift of the Spirit to the disciples is proof that the last days, i.e. the Messianic era foretold by the prophets, have arrived. Christians are living in the end time which will terminate with the glorious parousia of their Risen Lord.

Verse 19, which stigmatizes the evil teachers as worldly people (in the greek text *psychikoi*), devoid of the Spirit, who cause divisions in the communities, remind us of the distinction Paul makes in 1 Cor 2:13-15 between "the spiritual man" (*pneumatikos*) and "the unspiritual man" (*psychikos*). The unspiritual man, the *psychikos*, is a worldly man who does not have the Spirit of God and who judges everything by worldly standards and ridicules christian values as foolishness (1 Cor 2:14).The evil teachers, whom Jude condemns, boasted that they were "spirituals" who possessed a knowledge and wisdom superior to the religious knowledge and the wisdom given to the ordinary christian. Not so! says Jude. They are the *psychikoi*, the worldly people. Their licentious conduct shows that they do not have the Spirit of God. They live sensuous, animal lives, "following their own ungodly passions." Their pretended wisdom is that earthly, unspiritual (in the Greek text *psychike*), devilish wisdom of which James speaks (cf. Jas 3:15-16). The truly spiritual person who has received the wisdom from above is known by his/her good moral life (cf. Jas 3:13; Gal 5:16, 22-26).

Jude gives the faithful in verses 20-21 a program for the christian life. They must build themselves up on their most holy faith. Faith here probably means as in v.3 the doctrinal and moral truths which constitute the object of christian belief, i.e. "the faith which was once for all delivered to the saints." This sacred deposit, this faith, is the firm foundation of christianity. Holding fast to the faith handed on to them from the apostles, christians are to build themselves up, i.e. grow in personal holiness and contribute to the spiritual development and growth of the church. Jude's exhortation is similar to that of 1 Pt 2:5 "like living stones be yourselves built into a spiritual house." The picture of the faithful contributing through their growth in holiness to the construction of the community, which is in Paul's language "God's building" (1 Cor 3:9), suggests christian unity. The faithful construct and promote harmony; the evil teachers divide and demolish.

It is through prayer in the holy Spirit that the faithful receive the graces which enable them to build up "the house of God." It is also through prayer in the Spirit who pours forth God's love into their hearts (Rom 5:8) that they are inspired and moved to give themselves in love to God, to fulfill the first and basic commandment, "You shall love the Lord your God with all your heart, and with all your soul, and with all your mind" (Mt 22:37). Loved by God and loving Him the faithful await with patient hope the day of judgment when they will receive the merciful invitation of our Lord Jesus Christ to enter into the eternal life of the glorious Kingdom of God. Jude expresses beautifully the role of each person of the Trinity in the Christian life which is a life of faith, hope, and love. Note how the terms mercy, love, faith which are so prominent in the opening verses of the epistle (v.2-3) are all stressed here in the closing exhortation. By holding on to and "contending for the faith," and by prayer in the Holy Spirit the faithful will receive the blessing Jude desired for them in his greeting, "May mercy, peace, and love be multiplied to you"(v.2).

In verses 22-23 Jude advises the faithful how they should act toward the members of their communities who have succumbed, or are in proximate danger of succumbing, to the seduction of the evil teachers. He distinguishes three classes of endangered christians. First, there are some "who doubt" i.e. who are wavering between fidelity to the Lord and the seductive attractiveness of the false teaching. These people are still hestitating and have not yet made the decision to embrace the false teaching. The faithful, says Jude, should convince them; they should try by exhortation and instruction to keep them from embracing the vicious and erroneous teaching. Secondly, there are others, who in spite of the fact that they have succumbed to the persuasion of the false teachers, still offer some hope that they may be led back to the truth. The faithful should have pity for these poor wretches and attempt to snatch them out of the fire into which they have fallen. Two interpretations of the phrase "snatching them out of the fire" are possible. It may mean that the faithful should make every effort to withdraw the poor wretches from their association with the false teachers and to persuade them to return to the believing community. Probably the phrase is an Old Testament citation (e.g. cf. Zech 3:2) and the fire refers to the final, eschatological punishment, the gehenna of the gospels, a place of darkness and fire (cf. Mt 3:12; 5:29). By persuading their fellow brothers and sisters to return to the faith the christians will be saving them from hell. The third class are those who have not only embraced the erroneous teaching but who are also following the evil teachers in their licentiousness. The faithful must not associate with such persons for they are a dangerous occasion of sin. They should show mercy for them by praying that God in his mercy give them the grace of repentance. This seems to be the meaning of Jude's counsel: "have mercy with fear, hating even the garment spotted by the flesh." The last phrase clearly implies that the persons of this third class are living immoral lives indulging in licentious practices. The garment spotted by flesh is in the Greek text the *chiton*, the undergarment worn next to the body. This soiled garment is a metaphor which expresses moral corruption, so the faithful from fear of being corrupted must hate the immoral conduct of the fallen licentious christians. St. Ignatius of Antioch gave similar advice to the christians of Smyrna and Ephesus. He writes to the church of Smyrna: "Now I warn you of these things, beloved, knowing that you also are so minded. But I guard you in advance against beasts in the form of men, whom you must not only not receive, but if it is possible not even meet, but only pray for them, if perchance they may repent, difficult though that be — but

Jesus Christ who is our true life has the power over this"
(Ad. Smyrn. 4:1).

THE CONCLUDING DOXOLOGY.
24-25.

> **24** Now to him who is able to keep you from falling
> and to present you without blemish before the presence of
> his glory with rejoicing, **25** to the only God, our Saviour
> through Jesus Christ our Lord, be glory, majesty,
> dominion, and authority, before all time and now and
> for ever. Amen.

A solemn doxology, which has been called the most
beautiful in the New Testament, concludes this little
letter. Jude undoubtedly is citing a doxology used in the
liturgy of his church. He has skillfully adapted it to the
context of his epistle. The opening verse keeps in view the
purpose of the letter, the perseverance of his readers
whose faith and loyalty to Christ is endangered by the
seductive doctrine of evil teachers. Jude reminds his
readers that perseverance in the faith once for all delivered to the saints is a gift from God. Without his strength-
ening grace they will not, indeed cannot resist the evil
teachers and arrive unblemished at the glorious goal
to which they have been called in Christ. Only God our
Savior who accomplished his salvific plan and redeemed
us through Christ our Lord can bring them into the
presence of his glory where they will rejoice forever.
Some commentators see in the expresson "to the only
God" a rejection of the gnostic distinction between the
supreme Deity and the Demiurge who created the material world. But there is really no convincing evidence
that the false teachers condemned in the epistle held
this specific gnostic teaching. The expression "the only
God" occurs several times in the New Testament and
especially in doxologies (cf. Rom 16:27; 1 Tim 1:17;

also Jn 5:44; 17:3). This only God, who has saved us through Jesus Christ our Lord, possesses glory, majesty, dominion and authority from before time began and now and forever. To this magnificent expression of the transcendent majesty and eternity of God. Jude invites the assent of his readers: Amen – So it is! The modern reader will add his joyous assent with the little doxology of today's liturgy: "Glory to the Father, and to the Son, and to the Holy Spirit. As it was in the beginning, is now and will be forever. Amen."

EPILOGUE

THE EPISTLE OF JUDE opens a window giving us a view of the danger to faith to which some christian communities were exposed at the turn of the first century A.D. They had to content for the faith delivered to them by the Apostles against teachers who professed to be christians, but who embraced doctrines and practices that were pagan in origin. The situation of christians today is similar to that of Jude's addressees. Fidelity to the gospel demands that christians be on their guard against propagandists who, having compromised with the ambient secularism, attempt to persuade the followers of Christ that moral permissiveness, indeed licentious practices, are compatible with christian liberty.

This epistle also, because of the very problems it presents, has contributed to a balanced theology of biblical inspiration and truth. Until recent years many commentators attempted to obviate by evasive interpretations of the difficult passages Jude's use of apocryphal Jewish literature, his acceptance of Jewish legends, and especially his use of the Book of Enoch as sacred scripture.

In the inspired books of the Old and New Testaments we have God's word articulated in the words of men. These writers, like all human beings, were influenced in their thinking and expression by the culture and concepts of their day. They lived in a pre-scientific age. Many of their concepts, because of the limitations of their knowledge, were erroneous, indeed to us fantastic. God took these men as they were and through their writings communicated a very specific truth, namely "that truth which God wanted to put into the sacred writings for the sake of our salvation" (Vatican II, *Dei Verbum*).

Some commentators, protestant as well as catholic, seem to have defended the authenticity of Jude and to have denied his quite evident acceptance of the Jewish myth about the sexual sin of the angels and his recognition of the biblical authority of The Book of Enoch, because they could not reconcile pseudonymity (a reputable literary practice), nor his use of the Jewish apocrypha, with their concept of biblical inspiration and inerrancy. Jude has helped theologians come to a proper understanding of the specific truth of sacred scripture and led them to discard the misleading term "biblical inerrancy."

ANNOTATED READING LIST

Commentaries for the General Reader

Blackman, E.C., *The Epistle of James*. (Torch Bible Commentaries). Naperville, Il.: Alec E. Allenson, Inc., 1958.

James, M.R., *The Second Epistle General of Peter and the General Epistle of Jude*, With Introduction and Notes. (Cambridge Greek Testament For Schools And Colleges). Cambridge: The University Press 1912.
    Although written for students of the Greek text of the N.T., the general readers who knows no greek will find the section of the Introduction: Apocryphal Writings Quoted by Jude, pp. xl-xlviii, informative and interesting.

Leahy, Thomas W., S.J., *The Epistle of James*. (The Jerome Biblical Commentary #59) and *The Epistle of Jude* (#60). Englewood Cliffs, N.J.: Prentice Hall, Inc., 1968, pp. 369-380.

Moffatt, J., *The General Epistles*. (Moffatt New Testament Commentaries). New York & London, 1945.

Reicke, Bo, *The Epistles of James, Peter, and Jude*. (Anchor Bible #37). Garden City, N.Y.: Doubleday & Co., Inc., 1964.
    Reicke sees the Epistles of James, Peter, and Jude as preoccupied with the relations of christianity to the Roman Empire. They all, he maintains, condemn revolutionary tendencies and, like Paul (Rom 13) and the Pastoral Epistles, have "a remarkably positive attitude to state and society " (p. xxiii). "The recipients of the epistle of James appear to have been stirred to social discontent and political aggressiveness . . ." (p.6). He explains the situation of the churches

to which Jude is addressed by the same hypothesis: ". . . the current wave of apostasy is the work of seducers in the pay of foreign masters . . . the Christian community must have arrived at a level of some importance to be attractive to the magnates of the Roman Empire. Else why should extraordinary efforts be made to suborn Christians from their faith?" (pp. 191-192). This political hypothesis colors Reicke's interpretation of the epistles.

Tasker, R., *The General Epistle of James*. (Tyndale New Testament Commentaries). Grand Rapids, Mich.: Wm. B. Eerdmans Publ. Co., 1957.

Scholarly Commentaries of the Greek Text

Bigg, C., *The Epistles of St. Peter and St. Jude*. 2nd ed. (The International Critical Commentary). Edinburgh, 1910.

Chaine, J., *L'Épitre de Saint Jacques*. (Études bibliques). Paris: Libraire Lecoffre, J. Gabalda et Fils, 1927.

Dibelius, M. and Greeven, H., *Epistle of James*. (Hermeneia. A Critical and Historical Commentary on the Bible). Philadelphia, Pa.: Fortress Press, 1976.
    This is an excellent English translation of Dibelius' German Commentary. The treatment of the apparent contradiction between Jas. and the Pauline teaching on justification is excellent.

Mussner, F., *Der Jakobusbrief*. (Herders theologischer Kommentar zum Neuen Testament). Freiburg im Breisgau, 1964.
    This is now the best commentary by a Catholic scholar. But, like the earlier French commentator Chaine, he still defends the authenticity of Jas. His treatment of the parallels between Jas. and the Sayings of Jesus in the gospels, and his insights into the theology of Jas. are very good.

Ropes, J.H., *A Critical and Exegetical Commentary on the Epistle of St. James*. (The International Critical Commentary). Edinburgh, 1916.

Schelkle, K.H., *Die Petrusbriefe, der Judasbrief.* (Herders theologischer Kommentar zum Neuen Testament). Freiburg im Breisgau, 1961.

Informative Articles and Books

Brown, R.E., S.S., *Apocrypha; Dead Sea Scrolls; Other Jewish Literature.* (The Jerome Biblical Commentary # 68). Englewood Cliffs, N.J.: Prentice Hall, Inc., 1968. pp. 535-560, especially (I) Jewish Apocrypha; (II) The Enoch Literature; (XII) Assumption of Moses.

Charles, R.H., *Apocrypha and Pseudepigrapha of the Old Testament.* 2 vols. Oxford, 1913.
Vol. 2 gives an English translation of Enoch and of the fragments of The Assumption of Moses.

Gaster, T., *The Dead Sea Scriptures*, 3rd ed. New York: Doubleday/Anchor paperback, 1975.
An English translation of the Dead Sea Scrolls.

Vermes, G., *The Dead Sea Scrolls in English*, 2nd ed. Baltimore, Md.: Penguin Paperback, 1975.
For English translations of the First Epistle of Clement of Rome, of the Letters of Ignatius of Antioch, and of the Didache, which have been quoted in this commentary, the following two books are recommended.

Lake, K., editor and translator of *The Apostolic Fathers I.* (Harvard/Loeb Classical Library.) Cambridge and London, 1912. (This book also gives the Greek text.)

The Apostolic Fathers. Vol I. (The Fathers of the Church, A New Translation, L. Schopp, Editorial Director). New York: CIMA Publ. Co., Inc., 1947.

For The General Reader

Jeremias, J., "Paul and James" in Expository Times 66, 1954-1955, pp. 368-371.

Mac Rae, G.W., "Gnosis, Christian, and Gnosticism." (New Catholic Encyclopedia Vol. 1, pp. 522-528).

Michl, J., *Angels*. (New Catholic Encyclopedia, Vol. 6, pp. 506-514.)

Schnackenburg, R., *The Moral Teaching of the New Testament*. New York: Herder & Herder, 1965. Chapter Three: James, pp. 347-364.

On James and the Teaching of Jesus, the following items are informative.

Davies, W.D., *Setting of the Sermon on the Mount*. London and New York: Cambridge University Press, 1964, pp. 401-414.

Shepherd, M.H., *The Epistle of James and the Gospel of Matthew*. Journal of Biblical Literature 75, 1956, pp. 40-51.

The following monograph deserves the careful attention of scholars.

Hoppe, R., *Der theologische Hintergrund des Jakobusbriefes*. (Forschung zur Bibel #28). Würzburg: Echter Verlag, 1977.
   In view of the fact that many commentators following Dibelius maintain that there is nothing specifically christian in the ethical exhortation of Jas. and that it really contains no theology, this monograph is a provocative and important contribution to the scholarly literature on Jas. Hoppe adduces weighty evidence for the christian character of the epistle.